SMART BOOKS

STATES

How to use this book

This book has 200 QR (Quick Response) codes—those small patterned squares that link to Internet content. Use your smart phone, tablet, or PC's web cam to scan codes to access interactive games, quizzes, videos, and slideshows maintained on a secure, ad-free website hosted by Publications International, Ltd. Links to all content can also be found at http://qr.sdxi.com/smartbookstates.html. This content has been optimized for the screen size of smart phones. This product is not compatible with Windows® 7 phones. If your data plan is not unlimited, you may incur additional charges.

QUICK START

1. Open the app store on your device.

2. Download a free QR code scanner.

3. Open the scanner.

4. Point your device at a QR code in the book to watch videos, play games, learn state capitals, and more!

 Publications International, Ltd.

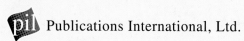

Publications International, Ltd.

Manufactured in China

8 7 6 5 4 3 2 1

Customer Service:
1-800-595-8484 or customer_service@pilbooks.com

ISBN-10: 1-4508-6384-1

www.pilbooks.com

ISBN-13: 978-1-4508-6384-1

Table of Contents

NEW ENGLAND

Vermont - 4
New Hampshire - 5
Rhode Island - 6
Connecticut - 7
Massachusetts - 8
Maine - 10

The Mid-Atlantic Region

Delaware - 12
Washington, D.C. - 13
Maryland - 14
New York - 16
New Jersey - 18
Pennsylvania - 20

THE MIDWEST

Illinois - 22
Missouri - 24
Indiana - 25
Ohio - 26
Minnesota - 28
Iowa - 29
Michigan - 30
Wisconsin - 32
Nebraska - 34
Kansas - 35
North Dakota - 36
South Dakota - 37

The South

Louisiana - 38
Florida - 40
Georgia - 42
South Carolina - 44
North Carolina - 45
Tennessee - 46
Kentucky - 48
Virginia - 50
West Virginia - 52
Arkansas - 54
Mississippi - 55
Alabama - 56

The Southwest

Oklahoma - 58
Texas - 60
New Mexico - 62
Arizona - 64

The Mountain States

Nevada - 66
Utah - 67
Idaho - 68
Montana - 69
Wyoming - 70
Colorado - 71

The Pacific Region

California - 72
Oregon - 74
Washington - 76
Alaska - 78
Hawaii - 79
Review - 80

Enjoy... VERMONT

What's the buzz?

In 1791, Vermont became the 14th state. It was the first one to enter the Union after the 13 original colonies. For 14 years before that, Vermont was its own country.

CAPITAL	Montpelier
POPULATION	626,431
AREA	9,216 square miles
STATE PIE	Apple pie
STATE BEVERAGE	Milk
STATE INSECT	Honeybee

This Place Is Really Sappy!

Have you eaten pancakes with real maple syrup? That syrup probably came from Vermont. Maple syrup is made from the sap of the sugar maple tree. The traditional way of collecting the sap is to drill a few holes into a tree and put a spout into each hole. The sap runs out through the spout.

How to tap the sap

· Burlington

Montpelier ★

· Rutland

DID YOU KNOW?

Vermont's capital, Montpelier, has the smallest population of any state capital in the United States.

Vermont is the second smallest state in population.

Forests cover more than three-fourths of the state.

Vermont is the largest producer of maple syrup in the United States.

Quiz time!

THE WHALE THAT LIVED IN THE LAND

In 1849, railroad workers were digging in the ground near Burlington, Vermont. They found some mysterious animal bones. The bones belonged to a fossil whom people called Charlotte. Charlotte is a whale that lived in Vermont when an ocean covered the area.

Vermont is noted for its covered bridges. It has more than 100 of them. The Windsor covered bridge connects Vermont to New Hampshire. It is 450 feet long, the longest in the country.

CAPITAL	Concord
POPULATION	1,318,194
AREA	8,952 square miles
STATE FLOWER	Purple lilac
STATE SPORT	Skiing
STATE FRUIT	Pumpkin

New Hampshire

Everything's nicer in...

Founded in 1623, New Hampshire was the third of the original 13 colonies. It is known for its independence. Its 221 towns are considered "little republics." Each year, they have town meetings. The townspeople elect their officials and vote on other matters of town business.

It's all downhill from here!

Into the woods

White Mountain National Forest

★Concord

Manchester.

Nashua.

Welcome to "New Quiz-shire!"

KEENE ON PUMPKINS

Pumpkins are so popular in New Hampshire that they were named the state fruit. The idea came from the Wells Memorial Elementary School in Harrisville, New Hampshire.

During the annual Keene Pumpkin Festival, there are plenty of pumpkins. The record for number of pumpkins lit was set in 2003, when 28,952 pumpkins were all glowing at once.

White Mountain National Forest attracts more visitors than Yosemite and Yellowstone national parks combined. Roughly 770,000 acres, it includes the Presidential Range. Its peaks are each named for an early U.S. president.

Experience...
MOUNT WASHINGTON

GET OUT THE VOTE!

Most states hold primary elections to help choose presidential candidates. New Hampshire's presidential primary is the first in the country. Since 1960, 62 percent of Democratic candidates and 69 percent of Republican candidates who won the N.H. primary went on the win their party's nomination.

The 6,288-foot Mount Washington is the highest peak in the northeastern United States. The mountain is also noted for its freakish weather. A year-round weather observatory has existed at its summit since 1870. Weather observers recorded a top wind speed of 231 miles per hour — the maximum wind gust ever recorded in the Northern and Western Hemispheres.

Little Rhody
RHODE ISLAND

CAPITAL	Providence
POPULATION	1,051,302
AREA	1,034 square miles
STATE DRINK	Coffee milk

State Bird: Rhode Island Red

The smallest of the 50 states, Rhode Island is only 48 miles long and 37 miles wide. You can easily drive across the entire state in an hour.

Because it's on the ocean, Rhode Island was a center of trade and shipping in the 1700s. It later became a center of industry in the 1800s. By 1860, Rhode Island was the most industrialized state in the nation.

Providence
★
Warwick

More Slater Mill

Samuel Slater built the first American cotton mill in Rhode Island based on his memory of English cotton mill designs.

WEIRD BUT TRUE

- In Rhode Island, it's considered an offense to throw pickle juice on a trolley.

- The state's official name is the State of Rhode Island and Providence Plantations.

- It's a crime to wrap a freshly caught fish in newspaper in Rhode Island.

- The world's largest bug resides in Providence, Rhode Island.

new england
pest control

RHODE ISLAND
QUIZ

6

CONNECTICUT

is full of surprises

CAPITAL	Hartford
POPULATION	3,580,709
AREA	4,842 square miles
NICKNAME	The Constitution State
STATE SHIP	Submarine
STATE SONG	"Yankee Doodle"

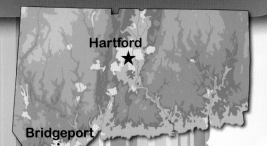

Hartford ★

Bridgeport

Tiny Connecticut is full of surprises. Long ago, volcanoes and glaciers created many different landscapes there. Today, its scenic forests, rolling hills, rich farmland, and sparkling beaches draw many visitors.

Connecticut became the fifth state in 1788. By then, this little state already had a big first. In 1639, it adopted the first written constitution based on the will of the people. For this reason, Connecticut is called "The Constitution State." It also had the nation's first public library and telephone exchange.

Letter scramble

A STRANGE SIGHT

Frog Bridge, Willimantic, Connecticut

With four frogs atop giant spools, this bridge pays tribute to the thread industry that was the backbone of the economy in the 19th century, and the infamous Battle of the Frogs of 1754, when the cries from drought-ravaged bullfrogs seriously alarmed locals during the French and Indian War.

More strange sights in Connecticut

Fun Facts

- Connecticut is the third-smallest state. It could fit inside Alaska 117 times.

- Connecticut is one of the most densely populated states. It has 738 people per square mile. The U.S. average is 87 people per square mile.

- The nation's oldest car ferry is in Rocky Hill, Connecticut.

See the car ferry in action

Connecticut's Hero

Nathan Hale is the official state hero of Connecticut. He was a teacher who became a spy for General George Washington during the Revolutionary War. Hale was hanged by British soldiers in 1776. His famous last words were "I only regret that I have but one life to lose for my country."

Welcome to the Bay State
MASSACHUSETTS

When European explorers first came to what is now Massachusetts, Algonquian tribes were already living there. Those first European settlers were two English groups looking for religious freedom. The Pilgrims sailed to America on the *Mayflower* and started Plymouth Colony in the southwestern part of the state in 1620. The other group was the Puritans. They founded a settlement in 1630 near what is now Boston. They called it the Massachusetts Bay Colony.

CAPITAL	Boston
POPULATION	6,587,536
AREA	7,800 square miles
STATE SPORT	Basketball
STATE DESSERT	Boston cream pie
STATE BERRY	Cranberry
STATE DOG	Boston terrier

Letter scramble

The Revolutionary War began in Massachusetts in 1775, when the British soldiers clashed with Colonial militias and minutemen. When the war ended, Massachusetts became the sixth state of the new nation. Factories opened and made textiles (cloth), furniture, and shoes. Now Massachusetts factory workers make scientific instruments, electrical equipment, books, and newspapers.

Minutemen and the Revolutionary War

Legend has it that Plymouth Rock was the place where the Pilgrims first set down in the New World.

Worcester

Springfield

Boston

Did You Know?

The first Thanksgiving was celebrated in 1621 in Plymouth, Massachusetts.

Massachusetts is home to the Basketball Hall of Fame and the Volleyball Hall of Fame. Both sports were invented in Massachusetts.

The Fig Newton was named after Newton, Massachusetts.

The world's largest stir-fry weighed 4,010 pounds and was prepared in Amherst.

The Bay State is the birthplace of four U.S. presidents: John Adams, John Quincy Adams, John F. Kennedy, and George H. W. Bush.

Harvest time at the bog

More Bay State stars

Most of the soil in Massachusetts is too thin and rocky for farming. But Massachusetts farmers do grow half of the cranberries in the United States.

Replica of the Mayflower, the ship that brought pilgrims to the New World

Quite a Catch!

Do you like fish? If you do, Massachusetts is the place for you. Fishers catch cod, flounder, scallops, clams, crabs, and lobster. Large fishing fleets bring their catches to the ports of Boston, New Bedford, and Gloucester. Did you know that Cape Cod, Massachusetts, got its name from the state fish—cod?

Massachusetts quiz

Only the last few miles of the marathon route are within Boston proper. If the race were named after the community with the most course miles, it would be called the Newton Marathon.

BOSTON MARATHON

The first Boston Marathon was held on April 19, 1897. Since then, the annual race has evolved and grown. Elite athletes from all over the world come to compete. About 500,000 spectators line the 26.2-mile course each year.

Best time (Men's Open): 2:03:01—Geoffrey Mutai, Kenya—set in 2011

Best time (Women's Open): 2:20:43—Margaret Okayo, Kenya—set in 2002

Best time (Men's Wheelchair): 1:18:25—Joshua Cassidy, Canada—set in 2012

Best time (Women's Wheelchair): 1:34:06—Wakaka Tsuchida, Japan—set in 2011

Most victories (Men's Wheelchair): 9—Ernst van Dyk, South Africa—set in 2010

Largest marathon: The Centennial Boston Marathon in 1996 had a record 35,868 finishers

Hottest temperature on race day: 100°F—recorded at the 1905 marathon

NEWTON
EST. 1630
Mile 21

Mile 21 marks the end of "Heartbreak Hill" in the Boston Marathon course.

Maine is on the move

MAINE

CAPITAL	Augusta
POPULATION	1,328,188
AREA	30,843 square miles
STATE ANIMAL	Moose

American Indians were the first settlers in Maine. The first Europeans came in the 1500s when the English, Portuguese, French, and Spanish traveled along the northeast coast of the United States. European explorers and would-be colonists hoped to develop trade for food and furs, to find wealth, and to discover a new passage to China and the Indies. The English explored the islands in the area and the mainland. They called it "Maine."

Moose puzzle

The first English colony was established in present-day Popham Beach, Maine, in 1607, the same year as the colony in Jamestown, Virginia. Popham Colony couldn't survive the harsh Maine winters, so Jamestown is regarded as America's first permanent settlement. Some later settlers lived in fishing villages. Others traded with Native peoples for furs. Many settlers cut timber from the forests. Fishing and timber are still important industries in Maine.

Augusta ★

Portland

Maine is famous for its wonderful lobster. Fishers must band the claws of lobsters so they can't pinch.

Lobster quiz

Lobster Trivia

- Lobsters have eight walking legs.
- To grip and shred food, lobsters use their crusher claw and pincher claw.
- Lobsters have three stomachs.
- To grow, lobsters shed, or molt, their exoskeletons.
- Despite their 20,000 eyes, lobsters have poor vision. They learn about their environment mostly through touch, taste, and smell.
- The largest lobster ever caught was 44 pounds!
- Lobsters can live to be 100 years old.

FAMOUS FIRSTS IN MAINE

The first ship built by English colonists in America was launched on the Kennebec River in 1607.

The nation's first sawmill was established near York in 1623.

York became the nation's first incorporated city in 1642.

The first naval battle of the Revolutionary War was fought off the coast of Machias, Maine, in 1775.

The first Veteran's Hospital in the United States, Togus, was founded in 1866.

ME

GOOD MORNING, Sunshine!

Maine is in the upper northeastern corner of the United States. It is farther east than any other state. Mainers are the first people in the United States to see the sun rise each day.

A Shining Point of Light

Lighthouses can be seen all along the coast of Maine. The Portland Head Light at Cape Elizabeth is one of the oldest lighthouses in America. It was built in 1791. Since then, its light has warned ships of dangerous rocks along the coast. A keeper used to live in the lighthouse and make sure the light always burned brightly so sailors could see it easily. Today, lighthouses have electric lights.

Maine quiz

DID YOU KNOW?

MAINE IS THE ONLY STATE WHOSE NAME HAS ONE SYLLABLE.

MAINE IS THE ONLY STATE THAT SHARES ITS BORDER WITH ONLY ONE OTHER STATE.

AUGUSTA IS THE MOST EASTERN CAPITAL CITY IN THE UNITED STATES.

MAINE ONCE MANUFACTURED 90% OF THE COUNTRY'S WOODEN TOOTHPICK SUPPLY.

MAINE CONTAINS 542,629 ACRES OF STATE AND NATIONAL PARKS.

MAINE'S BLUEBERRY CROP IS THE LARGEST IN THE NATION.

Acadia National Park

DECEMBER 7, 1787

The First State
Delaware

#1 FIRST!

CAPITAL	Dover
POPULATION	907,135
AREA	1,949 square miles
STATE BIRD	Blue Hen Chicken
STATE BUG	Ladybug
STATE MARINE ANIMAL	Horseshoe crab

Wilmington

Dover ★

Beginning in the 1630s, immigrants from Sweden settled near the mouth of the Delaware River and established the first permanent colony in the area. Delaware's unique location has made it a transportation center, and a much-contested colony. The Swedes, Dutch, and English fought for control of the area.

RIDING TOWARD INDEPENDENCE

In 1776, delegates from each of the 13 colonies got together to vote on whether to declare independence from Great Britain. Delaware delegate Caesar Rodney had to be in Philadelphia on July 2, 1776, to vote. But on July 1, he was still in Dover, Delaware, fighting those who favored remaining a colony. Rodney rode 80 miles on horseback through a stormy night and reached Philadelphia on July 2. Rodney represented Delaware, voted for independence, and made the vote unanimous.

BREAKAWAY COUNTIES

Delaware only has three counties. They all once belonged to the Pennsylvania Colony, but they split off to create their own state in 1776, when they also declared themselves free of British rule.

State symbol scramble

Did You Know?

- Delaware was the first state to ratify the federal Constitution on December 7, 1787, becoming the first state in the Union.

- Because Delaware bordered the free state of Pennsylvania, Wilmington was an important last stop on the Underground Railroad for many escaping slaves.

- Settlers from Sweden and Finland built America's first log cabins in Delaware.

- Delaware is the second smallest state and the only state without a national park.

- Wilmington is home to the World's Largest Frying Pan. Built in 1950 for the Delmarva Chicken Festival, the frying pan is 10 feet in diameter.

- In 1880, Rehoboth Beach held one of the first beauty contests in the U.S. Thomas Edison was one of the three judges.

Delaware quiz

DISTRICT OF COLUMBIA

Our country's capital

POPULATION	617,996
AREA	61 square miles
OFFICIAL FLOWER	American beauty rose
OFFICIAL BIRD	Wood thrush

Washington, D.C.

D.C. quiz

Washington, D.C., serves as our nation's capital. Located in the District of Columbia, Washington is the only U.S. city that isn't part of a state. Instead, it belongs to the citizens of all the states.

When Europeans arrived in the early 1600s, Piscataway Indians already lived there. By 1700, all the land had been divided among the new settlers, and few Piscataway people remained. In 1790, Congress chose the area to be the country's capital. Washington has many beautiful public buildings, museums, monuments, fountains, and parks.

See more D.C. sights

A Home Fit for a President

President George Washington and city planner Pierre L'Enfant chose the site for the presidential residence, now listed at 1600 Pennsylvania Avenue. Irish-born architect James Hoban designed the White House after winning a contest. Construction began in 1792 and was not yet completed in 1800 when President John Adams and his wife, Abigail, became the first residents. During the War of 1812, the British set fire to the White House. James Hoban was appointed to rebuild it. Encompassing roughly 55,000 square feet, the White House has 132 rooms, including 35 bathrooms and 16 family and guest rooms.

White House trivia

More than you can imagine
Maryland

Maryland is a small state with an unusual shape. The Chesapeake Bay almost cuts the state in half. The Chesapeake Bay is the largest estuary in the country. An estuary is a place where saltwater meets freshwater. The Chesapeake Bay saltwater comes from the Atlantic Ocean. The freshwater comes from rivers that flow into the bay.

Calico cat

Maryland fish match

CAPITAL	Annapolis
POPULATION	5,828,289
AREA	9,707 square miles
STATE CAT	Calico
STATE FISH	Rockfish (aka striped bass)

Maryland has a lot of water. The Chesapeake Bay runs right down the middle of the state.

- Baltimore
- ★ Annapolis

Maryland began as a colony founded on religious freedom. During the Revolutionary War, Marylanders built ships and cannons for the colonial army. In 1788, Maryland became the seventh state.

Today, most Marylanders work in service industries. Many work for the federal government (Maryland is next to Washington, D.C.). Almost all Marylanders live in or near a city. Baltimore is the largest city and the major commercial center.

One of the fiercest battles of the Civil War was fought in Maryland. The Battle of Antietam was a clash between North and South that changed the course of the Civil War, helped free over four million Americans, and still ranks as the bloodiest one-day battle in American history.

Battle of Antietam

AN UNDERGROUND HERO

Harriet Tubman was born a slave on a Maryland plantation. She escaped north in 1849 but returned to lead other slaves to freedom. She was a conductor on the Underground Railroad, a secret network that helped slaves escape to the free states or Canada. Tubman made 19 rescue trips and helped about 300 slaves escape. She was never caught, despite many close calls.

Maryland quiz

A National Anthem Is Born

During the War of 1812, the British tried to capture the port of Baltimore and Fort McHenry. Francis Scott Key, an American lawyer, witnessed the battle. The battle lasted all night until the sounds of fighting suddenly stopped just before morning. Key thought the battle had been lost. When the sun came up, Key saw the American flag still waving high above the fort. He knew then that the American troops had successfully held off the British. Key was so inspired, he wrote a poem that later became the words to our national anthem, "The Star-Spangled Banner."

Fort McHenry's flag

O say can you see, by the dawn's early light,
What so proudly we hail'd at the twilight's last gleaming,
Whose broad stripes and bright stars through the perilous fight
O'er the ramparts we watch'd were so gallantly streaming?
And the rockets' red glare, the bombs bursting in air,
Gave proof through the night that our flag was still there,
O say does that star-spangled banner yet wave
O'er the land of the free and the home of the brave?

NEW YORK

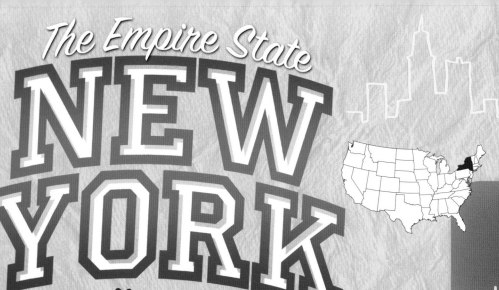

CAPITAL	Albany
POPULATION	19,465,197
AREA	47,126 square miles
LARGEST CITY	New York City

New York in a Nutshell

New York was one of the original 13 colonies to declare independence in 1776. Almost one third of the battles fought during the Revolutionary War were fought in New York. The state grew rapidly after 1814. Millions of immigrants came from Europe and settled in the state or continued west. The state developed good transportation; it could move people and goods by road, river, or the Erie Canal. By the 1830s, its railroad network was beginning to tie together its cities, towns, and farms. New York soon had more people than any other state. It led the nation in manufacturing, trade, and finance. New York City, which has a great natural harbor, became the busiest port in the world. New York is still a leader in finance, fashion, and arts and entertainment. Where New York City leads, the rest of the nation usually follows.

STATE BIRD: EASTERN BLUEBIRD

WHAT DO YOU KNOW ABOUT NEW YORK?

Niagara Falls • Rochester
• Buffalo
Albany ★

New York City

OUR LADY OF LIBERTY

The Statue of Liberty was placed on an island in New York harbor in 1886. Liberty Enlightening the World (the statue's official name) was a gift from the people of France to the people of the United States. It became a welcoming figure for generations of immigrants arriving in New York.

What's up with the Big Apple?

AMERICA'S FIRST WATER HIGHWAY

In 1825, the Erie Canal connected Albany on the Hudson River to Buffalo on Lake Erie. Immigrants could travel west, paying only a few cents per mile. Commercial goods traveled faster and more cheaply between the Atlantic Ocean and the Great Lakes.

TRAVEL BY... PACKET BOAT?

Lake Ontario

ERIE CANAL

Rochester
Buffalo
Syracuse
Utica
Mohawk

Lake Erie

Albany

Hudson

New York City

How big can one park get?

DAREDEVILS OF THE FALLS

New York Fun Facts

722
miles of subway track in New York City

HIGHEST WATERFALL
Taughannock Falls, 215 feet

544
number of toy stores

33
number of amusement parks

STATE NICKNAME
The Empire State

STATE BEVERAGE
milk

80 MILES
DISTANCE YOU CAN SEE FROM THE OBSERVATION DECK OF THE EMPIRE STATE BUILDING

A CAPITAL CONNECTION

The Unites States has had more than one capital. From 1785 to 1790 New York City was the capital of the nation!

Federal Hall, New York

New Jersey
The Garden State

CAPITAL	Trenton
POPULATION	8,821,155
AREA	7,354 square miles
PEOPLE PER SQUARE MILE	1,196

New Jersey geography

Newark
Jersey City
Trenton
Pine Barrens
Atlantic City

New Jersey became the third state in 1787. The state quickly grew into a powerhouse of the Industrial Revolution. In the early 1800s, factories began to spring up, leading to urban growth and improved transportation. Paterson was known for its textiles. Trenton made clay, iron, and steel products. Other important manufacturing centers included Newark, Camden, Elizabeth, Jersey City, and Passaic.

Despite all of its cities, New Jersey's nickname is the "Garden State." Today, more than 17 percent of the land in New Jersey is farmland. Over 40 percent of the state's agricultural production is from greenhouse and nursery products. It is also a major producer of fruits like apples, peaches, and strawberries. It ranks second in blueberry production and third in cranberry production.

Hoboken is one of many densely populated cities in northeastern New Jersey.

STROLLING THE BOARDWALK

Conceived in 1870, Atlantic City's Boardwalk was built to keep sand out of local hotels. By 1896, it was four miles long and sixty feet wide. Its charm helped turn Atlantic City into a thriving resort area. The Boardwalk is now open 24 hours a day and has added casinos to its attractions.

NEW JERSEY FIRSTS

SO LITTLE SPACE, SO MANY PEOPLE!

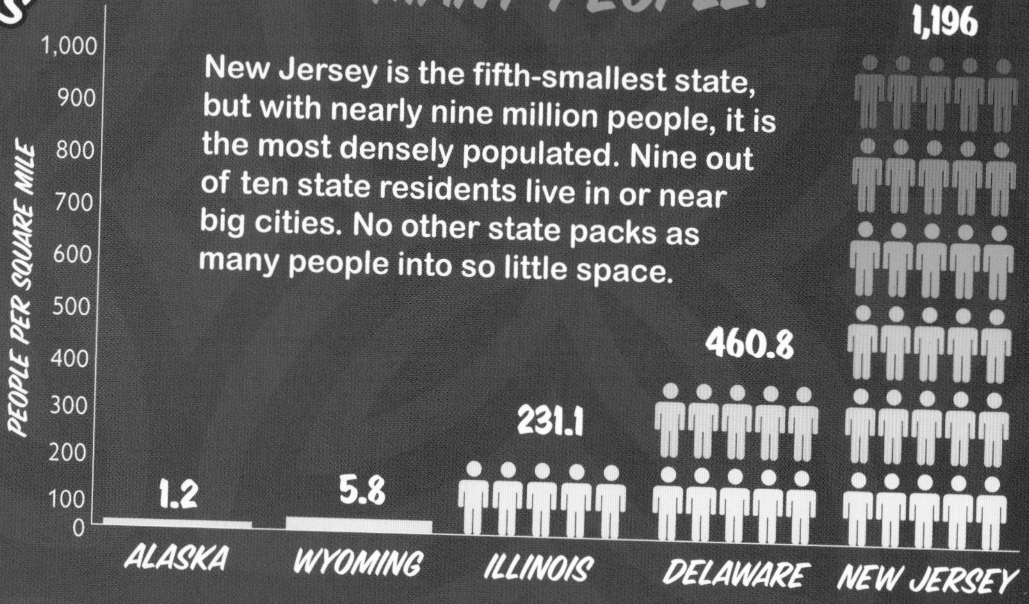

New Jersey is the fifth-smallest state, but with nearly nine million people, it is the most densely populated. Nine out of ten state residents live in or near big cities. No other state packs as many people into so little space.

PEOPLE PER SQUARE MILE

State	People per square mile
ALASKA	1.2
WYOMING	5.8
ILLINOIS	231.1
DELAWARE	460.8
NEW JERSEY	1,196

Jersey letter jumble

The Pine Barrens

New Jersey may be heavily urbanized, but it is also home to the Pinelands National Reserve. This immense area contains over one million acres of wetlands and forest. It represents 22 percent of the state's total land area.

Home of the bright idea

THE JERSEY... Devil?

Many states have a few legends or rumors about mysterious creatures lurking in backwaters and unpopulated regions. The Pine Barrens have the Jersey Devil. The 300-year old legend describes a creature that resembles a kangaroo, ostrich, or two-legged goat, with wings and possibly a tail!

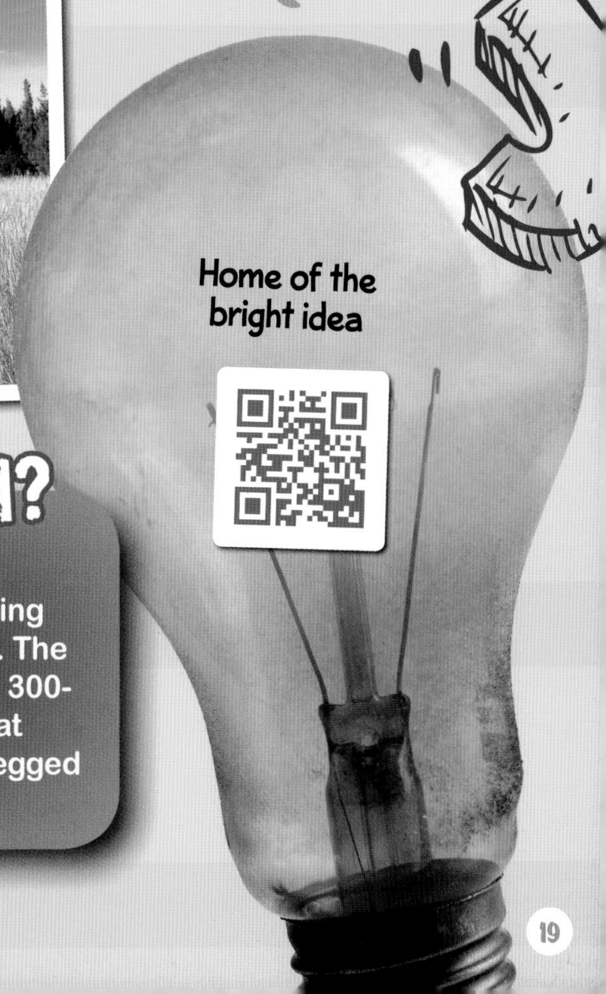

Pennsylvania

The Keystone State

CAPITAL	Harrisburg
POPULATION	12,742,886
AREA	44,742 square miles
YEAR OF STATEHOOD	1787
STATE DOG	Great Dane

Appalachian Mountains

Pittsburgh

Harrisburg

Philadelphia

Pennsylvania quiz

In 1681, King Charles of England gave William Penn a massive land grant to pay for an old debt. This land included much of present-day Delaware, New Jersey, and Pennsylvania. Penn arrived in 1682 and began to plan the city of Philadelphia. He wanted the colony to provide freedom for all religions. He also wanted it to be profitable. It became both, and was soon one of the most important colonies. The nation's leaders wrote the Declaration of Independence and the U.S. Constitution in Philadelphia, Pennsylvania.

Independence Hall

The seeds of liberty were sown in Philadelphia's Independence Hall. The Declaration of Independence was signed here in 1776. It was first read in public in Independence Square a few days after its signing. The famous Liberty Bell, which is now on display in a pavilion across from the hall, was rung to announce the public reading.

Liberty Bell

The Liberty Bell weighs 2,080 pounds.

FLIGHT 93

On September 11, 2001, al Qaeda terrorists hijacked four airplanes, flying two airplanes into the World Trade Center in New York City and a third plane into the Pentagon in Arlington, Virginia. The fourth hijacked airplane, United Airlines Flight 93, crashed into an open field in Somerset County, Pennsylvania. Because of the actions of the passengers and crew, Flight 93 was the only one of the four hijacked planes that didn't reach the terrorists' intended target.

The story of Flight 93

Did you know?

- Pennsylvanian Milton Hershey founded the Hershey Chocolate Company and later the company town of Hershey, Pennsylvania.

- New Kensington native Stephanie Kwolek invented Kevlar, a synthetic material five times as strong as steel, which is used in bullet-proof vests.

- Philadelphia is home to the cheesesteak sandwich and soft pretzels.

- Kennett Square is known as the Mushroom Capital of the World.

PA people matching game

MUMMERS PARADE

The Mummers Parade, a Philadelphia institution that dates back to the late 1700s, was started by Swedish immigrants. The annual New Year's Day parade boasts extravagant costumes, string band and brass band music, dancing clowns, and elaborate floats. Many of Philadelphia's Mummers spend the entire year practicing dance and band routines and constructing their elaborate costumes.

Mummers Parade pictures

PENNSYLVANIA DUTCH

Southeastern Pennsylvania is home to a group of people called the Pennsylvania Dutch. The ancestors of the Pennsylvania Dutch weren't really Dutch. They were German. The name comes from mispronouncing the German word Deutsch, which means "German." One group of Pennsylvania Dutch is the Amish. The Amish use horse-drawn buggies and plows. They don't have phones, electricity, or cars. Farming, carpentry, and construction are common jobs. Peace and nonviolence are important in Amish life.

Amish horse-drawn buggies are a common sight in parts of Pennsylvania.

21

Welcome to... ILLINOIS

ILLINOIS

Illinois became the 21st state on December 3, 1818. People came to Illinois to farm, dig canals, build railroads, and work in the mills, factories, and stockyards. Chicago, only a tiny trading post in 1818, became the largest city in Illinois and is now the third-largest city in the United States.

Chicago

Springfield

CAPITAL	Springfield
POPULATION	12,869,257
AREA	55,519 square miles
STATE DANCE	Square dance
STATE BIRD	Northern cardinal
STATE TREE	White oak
STATE INSECT	Monarch butterfly
STATE SNACK	Popcorn
STATE FOSSIL	"Tully Monster"

Find out how much you know about "The Land of Lincoln!"

HONEST ABE

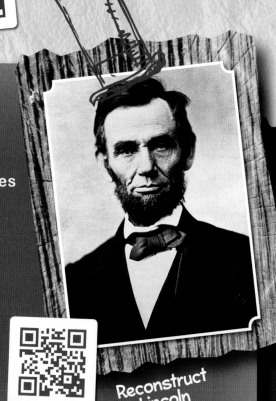

Abraham Lincoln was born in Kentucky, but he lived most of his life in Illinois. He was elected the 16th President of the United States in 1860. Lincoln signed the Emancipation Proclamation in 1863, which called for an end to slavery. The 13th Amendment to the Constitution officially abolished slavery in 1865. Illinois was the first state to ratify the amendment.

He was the tallest U.S. president at 6 ft. 4 in.

He created a national banking system, resulting in a standardized currency.

He was the first U.S. president to have a beard.

He was the first U.S. president to be assassinated.

Reconstruct Lincoln

The Tri-State Tornado

The worst tornado in U.S. history hit Missouri, Illinois, and Indiana on March 18, 1925. Illinois was hit hardest, with the town of Murphysboro suffering the worst devastation.

Total death toll: 695

Fujita scale rating: F5
(The highest a tornado can get!)

Average speed: 66 mph

Path traveled: 219 miles

Property damage: $16.5 million
(Which would be $1.7 billion in today's dollars!)

After the storm

FAMOUS ILLINOIS FIRSTS

First skyscraper—1885
(It was only 10 stories tall!)

First Ferris wheel—1893

First elevated railway—1892

First McDonald's restaurant—1955

AMAZING & UNUSUAL ILLINOIS

More amazing sights

Superman—Metropolis, Illinois
This 15-foot bronze in Superman's hometown of Metropolis, Illinois, celebrates its favorite local hero.

Tower of Pisa replica—Niles, Illinois
In 1934, a businessman built a recreation park with this half-size replica of the Leaning Tower of Pisa to cover the pool's water tank.

World's Largest Catsup Bottle—Collinsville, Illinois
The World's Largest Catsup Bottle Festival is held every summer for food and fun (and, of course, catsup tasting).

From the top of **Willis Tower,** you can see four states: **Illinois, Indiana, Wisconsin, & Michigan.**

...in beautiful

CHICAGO

America's tallest building

Show me... MISSOURI

Two great rivers run through Missouri—the Mississippi River and the Missouri River. These rivers and Missouri's central location make the state a transportation center.

In 1673, French explorers Father Jacques Marquette and Louis Joliet marked the place where the Mississippi and Missouri rivers meet. French trappers and fur traders soon set up posts along the Missouri River. France and Spain in turn owned the land, as pioneers explored and settled there.

In 1803, the U.S. government bought the Missouri area as part of the Louisiana Purchase. Meriwether Lewis and William Clark began their journey to explore the Northwest on the Missouri River near St. Louis. In time, the territory became the gateway to the West.

CAPITAL	Jefferson City
POPULATION	6,010,688
AREA	68,742 square miles
STATE DESSERT	Ice cream cone
STATE ANIMAL	Missouri mule
STATE AMPHIBIAN	Bullfrog

Missouri memory game

Kansas City
Jefferson City
St. Louis

Extreme Weather

Joplin tornado

Missouri has had its share of extreme weather, including some of the largest earthquakes, deadliest tornadoes, and most destructive floods our nation has ever seen. The tornado that hit Joplin, Missouri, on May 22, 2011, was the third-deadliest tornado in U.S. history.

Missouri's past as the gateway to the West is represented by the Gateway Arch in St. Louis. It's the country's tallest monument.

1835 · M. TWAIN · 1910

MARK TWAIN

One of the most famous Missourians was Mark Twain. He grew up in Hannibal, Missouri, a town on the Mississippi River. He wrote about his experiences as a riverboat pilot in the book *Life on the Mississippi*. People still go to Hannibal to see his childhood home and a cave that he described in *Tom Sawyer*.

Missouri caves

Indiana
THE CROSSROADS OF AMERICA

CAPITAL	Indianapolis
POPULATION	6,516,922
AREA	35,826 square miles
NICKNAME	The Hoosier State
STATE MOTTO	The Crossroads of America
STATE FLOWER	Peony

The Miami, Illini, and Shawnee Indians were the first inhabitants of Indiana. Both the French and the British ruled the area before the United States gained control in 1783. As more white settlers moved into the area, Native peoples were pushed father west. Though the state's name means "Land of Indians," few American Indians remain in Indiana.

When Indiana became a state in 1816, much of it was still wilderness. Pioneers cleared the land for farming. They built houses, stores, and schools. Indiana was the first state to call for free public schools for its children. The people also built roads, canals, and railroads. These are what helped make Indiana a crossroads, which gave the state its motto.

INDY 500

Since it opened in 1909, the Indianapolis Motor Speedway has held 93 Indianapolis 500 races, 16 Brickyard 400 NASCAR events, and 8 United States Grand Prix Formula One events.

The Indianapolis Motor Speedway is the world's largest spectator sporting facility, with more than 250,000 permanent seats.

The first event held at the Speedway was a helium gas-filled balloon competition.

The Speedway infield covers 253 acres. The Roman Colosseum could fit inside the oval 42 times.

Fastest time to complete the Indy 500: 2 hours 41 minutes 18.404 seconds—set by Arie Luyendyk in 1990. His average winning speed was 185.981 mph.

Closest margin of victory at the Indy 500: 0.043 of a second—Al Unser Jr. over Scott Goodyear in 1992

First woman to drive the Indy 500: Janet Guthrie in 1977

Fort Wayne•

★Indianapolis

Evansville

Indy 500 flag game

McDonald's

OHIO
The Heart of It All

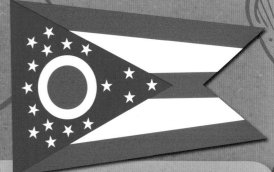

During the 1700s, the English, French, and American Indians fought over the land that is now Ohio. The French gave up their claim in 1763. In 1795, the Native people ceded much of their lands to the U.S. government.

Many of Ohio's first settlers came from the eastern states. New Englanders founded Ohio's first town, Marietta, in 1788. In the 1800s, many people from other countries came to Ohio. Many African-Americans came to Ohio, too. Today, Ohio is the seventh most populated state.

CAPITAL	Columbus
POPULATION	11,544,951
AREA	40,861 square miles
STATE BEVERAGE	Tomato juice
STATE NICKNAME	The Buckeye State

Cleveland

Columbus ★

Cincinnati

Ohio quiz

Mother of Presidents

Ohio is sometimes called the Mother of Presidents. Seven U.S. presidents were born in Ohio.

Ulysses S. Grant
born in Point Pleasant, Ohio

Warren G. Harding
born in Blooming Grove, Ohio

William McKinley
born in Niles, Ohio

William H. Taft
born in Cincinnati, Ohio

Rutherford B. Hayes
born in Delaware, Ohio

James A. Garfield
born in Orange, Ohio

Benjamin Harrison
born in North Bend, Ohio

PRESIDENT MATCH-UP GAME

Born in
THE BUCKEYE STATE

Apollo 11 video

Annie Oakley

At age 15, Ohio native Annie Oakley won a shooting contest against famous marksman Frank Butler, whom she later married. The couple joined Buffalo Bill Cody's Wild West Show in 1885, and she wowed audiences with her feats of marksmanship. Sioux Indian Chief Sitting Bull nicknamed her "Little Sure Shot" because she never missed a shot.

Thomas Edison films
Annie Oakley

Neil Armstrong

Astronaut Neil Armstrong was commander of *Apollo 11* and the first person to set foot on the moon. After retiring from NASA, the Wapakoneta native taught aeronautical engineering at the University of Cincinnati. In 1986, President Ronald Reagan named him vice chairman of the panel that investigated the explosion of the space shuttle *Challenger*, which killed seven, including another Ohioan, astronaut Judith Resnik.

CY YOUNG

Born in Gilmore, Ohio, Denton "Cy" Young began his career with the Cleveland Spiders. Young earned the nickname "Cy," short for "cyclone," after throwing a ball with such force that it shattered a fence into pieces. In 1904, he pitched the American League's first perfect game (no opposing batter reached first base). Young holds the record for winning the most games (511), including 76 shutouts, and 3 no-hit games. The Cy Young Award is given annually in his honor to the best pitcher in each major league.

Cy Young winners

Ohio Inventions

1878   Dayton resident James Ritty develops the first cash register.

1888   Ohio-born inventor Thomas Edison patents the kinetoscope, an early motion picture camera.

1907   James Murray Spangler, a janitor from Canton, invents the vacuum cleaner.

1923   Cleveland entrepreneur Garret Morgan patents his invention, the traffic light.

1938   Roy J. Plunkett, of New Carlisle, invents Teflon.

MINNESOTA
The Land of 10,000 Lakes

Minnesota is known for its waters and its woods. One of Minnesota's nicknames is "Land of 10,000 Lakes." Minnesota actually has more than 15,000 lakes, which were carved by glaciers beginning about two million years ago.

Quiet pine forests stretch for many miles in Minnesota. But rugged Minnesota has resources as well as pretty scenery. It leads the nation in iron ore production. About two million Christmas trees come from Minnesota each year. Southern Minnesota has rich farmland. It produces lots of sugar beets, dairy cattle, and corn.

Minnesota is famous for its cold weather. The coldest temperature recorded in Minnesota was -60°F, the fifth coldest temperature recorded in the country. Minnesotans love warm- and cold-weather sports. Waterskiing was invented in Minnesota.

WHAT DO YOU KNOW ABOUT MINNESOTA?

CAPITAL	St. Paul
POPULATION	5,344,861
AREA	79,626 square miles
STATE SPORT	Ice hockey
STATE MUFFIN	Blueberry muffin

Lake Itasca
Duluth
Minneapolis
★ St. Paul

MIGHTY MISSISSIPPI

The mighty Mississippi, one of our nation's biggest and longest rivers, begins at Lake Itasca in Minnesota. It is only inches deep and a few feet wide there.

Mississippi headwaters

More Minnesota sights

IRON MAN

The 81-foot-tall *Iron Man* statue stands across from the Ironworld Discovery Center in Chisholm. Exhibits there explore Minnesota's involvement in the iron mining industry. Open-pit mining was a big business in Minnesota until the mid-1970s. As the iron deposits ran out, another form of mining replaced it, which extracts iron in a complicated mechanized process.

IOWA

welcomes you

IOWA

CAPITAL	Des Moines
POPULATION	3,062,309
AREA	55,857 square miles
STATE NICKNAME	The Hawkeye State
STATE BIRD	Eastern goldfinch

Goldfinch puzzle

American Indians were the first Iowans. They made their homes near Iowa's great rivers: the Mississippi in the east and the Missouri in the west. They traveled along the rivers by canoe. They farmed and hunted deer and buffalo. When settlers moved west during the 1800s, American Indians were forced from their land.

Farming has always been important to Iowa's economy. Iowa farmers grow corn and raise hogs, beef and dairy cattle, sheep, turkeys, and horses. Many Iowans work in food-processing plants making canned ham, breakfast sausage, and popcorn. Some Iowans work in factories that make farm machinery.

Cedar Rapids

Davenport

Des Moines

Iowa by the numbers

IOWA STATE FAIR

When it comes to state fairs, Iowa brings home the blue ribbon. The Iowa State Fair is the single largest event in the state of Iowa, attracting more than a million people a year. Visitors to the 445-acre fairgrounds in Des Moines can find just about anything there. In addition to rides, games, concerts, livestock shows, and unique contests like the ugliest cake, the Iowa State Fair boasts nearly 200 food stands and more than 50 food items served on a stick.

IN 2011, IOWA PRODUCED 2.36 BILLION BUSHELS OF CORN.

State fair slideshow

29

MICHIGAN

CAPITAL	Lansing
POPULATION	9,876,187
AREA	56,539 square miles
STATE BIRD	Robin
STATE STONE	Petoskey stone

What's a Petoskey stone?

Mackinac Island

Sleeping Bear Dunes National Lakeshore

Lansing ★ Detroit

Battle Creek

In the 1600s, French explorers and fur traders came to Michigan and established forts and settlements there. They traded with the Ottawa, Ojibwe, and Potawatomi. After the French and Indian War, control of the area went to the British in 1763. Later, after the American Revolutionary War, Britain passed control of the area to the United States. Michigan became a territory in 1805. When the Erie Canal opened in 1825, settlement and trade increased. Michigan became the 26th state in 1837. Mining, farming, and logging helped build the area.

World War II

MOTOR CITY

Many American automobile companies are headquartered in the Detroit area, including General Motors, Chrysler, and Ford. In 1913, Henry Ford revolutionized the automobile industry when he began using the moving assembly line in his plants. In an autobiography, he wrote that he had once said about the Model T: "Any customer can have a car painted any color that he wants so long as it is black." This was because the black paint dried the fastest.

Ambassador Bridge

WU 08V

HIGHER EDUCATION

Both the University of Michigan and Michigan State University have played a big role in higher education in the U.S. They have a famous rivalry, too!

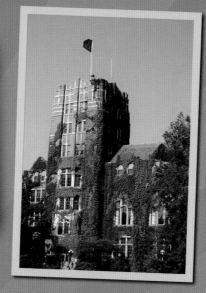

The University of Michigan dates back to 1817, before Michigan was a state! In 1960, when John F. Kennedy was campaigning for president, he made a stop at the University of Michigan. In a speech, he proposed that college students serve around the globe. This idea became the Peace Corps.

MACKINAC ISLAND

In the 1860s, the federal government started turning over federal land to states so that they could create colleges and universities. These land-grant institutions focused on practical subjects like agriculture and engineering. Michigan State University was founded in 1855 by the state. It acted as a model for these later land-grant colleges.

WHAT DO YOU KNOW?

On Mackinac Island, cars aren't allowed. Visitors arrive by ferry or plane, and use bikes and horse-drawn taxis while they're on the island.

The Great Lakes state

CEREAL CITY

Sleeping Bear Dunes

Sleeping Bear Dunes National Lakeshore has some of the largest sand dunes in the world. They're found on the shores of Lake Michigan, one of Michigan's four Great Lakes.

In the late 1800s, a doctor named John ran a health institute in Battle Creek with the help of his brother Will. One of the healthy foods that Will served the patients was a new breakfast cereal. In 1906, Will began a company, the Battle Creek Toasted Corn Flake Company, to sell the cereal. Later the company changed its name to reflect Will's last name: Kellogg. Kellogg's is still based in Battle Creek today.

Forward WISCONSIN →

WISCONSIN

1848

CAPITAL	Madison
POPULATION	5,711,767
AREA	54,158 square miles
STATE DOMESTICATED ANIMAL	Dairy cow
STATE ANIMAL	Badger

In the 1600s, the Ho Chunk, Ojibwe, and Menominee tribes were among the first groups to meet French explorers. In the century that followed, French and English fur traders came to the area, as well as some American Indian tribes that were being pushed west. After the Revolutionary War, the area became part of United States territory. However, few Americans settled in the region until after the War of 1812. Many of the first settlers were lead miners.

In 1848, Wisconsin became the 30th state. The first farmers in the state planted wheat. However, as soil became worn out, people in the new state turned to dairy farming.

The Badger State

Door County

Wisconsin River

Baraboo

Milwaukee

★ Madison

A State of Circuses

In 1884, the Ringling Brothers Circus put on their first show in the city of Baraboo. They also wintered there for many years. In fact, a number of circus acts spent their winters in Wisconsin. Baraboo's Circus World Museum honors that part of the state's history.

WHAT DO YOU KNOW?

WATERY WISCONSIN

The Mississippi River runs along part of Wisconsin's western boundary, and the Wisconsin River runs through the state. Lake Superior and Lake Michigan both border Wisconsin, and the state contains thousands of smaller lakes. So it's no surprise that the National Fresh Water Fishing Hall of Fame is found in Wisconsin.

Door County

Door County is famous for its beaches, its lighthouses, and its traditional fish boils. Whitefish are cooked with onions and potatoes over an open fire.

Eating in Wisconsin

WISCONSIN FIRSTS

Some things that became common throughout the U.S. had their start in Wisconsin.

WHAT: America's first kindergarten
WHEN: 1856
WHERE: Watertown

WHAT: The modern typewriter with the QWERTY keyboard used with today's computers
WHEN: 1868
WHERE: Milwaukee

WHAT: The round silo
WHEN: 1891
WHERE: University of Wisconsin-Madison

The round silo

Strange Architecture

The House on the Rock opened in 1959 and has been entertaining tourists since. Visitors can see everything from detailed dollhouses to replicas of armor to a large indoor carousel with 269 animals.

The dairy industry is still very important in Wisconsin. It is the top state in cheese production!

It's nice to be in...
Nebraska

CAPITAL	Lincoln
POPULATION	1,842,641
AREA	76,824 square miles
STATE FISH	Channel catfish
STATE ROCK	Prairie agate

Chimney Rock

Omaha

Lincoln

Both Nebraska and Kansas were part of the 1803 Louisiana Purchase. American settlement of the West increased in the 1840s and 1850s, and many of the trails that pioneers followed went through Nebraska. In the 1860s, many people settled in Nebraska because of the Homestead Act. The federal government wanted people to set up farms. The act said that pioneers who claimed a piece of land, lived on it for five years, and improved it would then own the land for free. Nebraska became a state in 1867.

Arbor Day was first celebrated in Nebraska.

Find out more!

Building Blocks

Because few trees were found on the plains, many settlers built their homes with sod instead of timber. They made blocks out of grass and dirt from the prairie. Few of these houses survive today.

Nebraska knowledge

Dowse Sod House was built in 1900.

A MODERN MONUMENT

Drivers on Highway 87 can stop by *Carhenge*, a set of 38 automobiles, all painted gray. The cars are set up to mimic the arrangement of standing stones of Stonehenge in England.

A NATURAL LANDMARK

Pioneers traveling to or through Nebraska used Chimney Rock as a reference point along the way. It's pictured on the state quarter.

KANSAS

CAPITAL	Topeka
POPULATION	2,871,238
AREA	81,759 square miles
STATE AMPHIBIAN	Barred tiger salamander
STATE SONG	"Home on the Range"

Hear the state song

Abilene

Topeka

Wichita

There's no place like..
Kansas

Test your Kansas knowledge

In 1854, the Kansas-Nebraska Act was passed. It organized Kansas Territory and Nebraska Territory so Americans could set up homesteads and eventually form states. At the time, people were arguing about slavery. The act said that the whites who settled in Kansas Territory could decide whether it would be a slave state or a free state. Proslavery and antislavery settlers rushed to the area. There were many fights. At one point, there were even two governments. In 1861, Kansas entered the Union as a free state.

THE MAN FROM ABILENE

BIG BRUTUS

This giant earth-moving shovel was used in coal mines from 1962 to 1974. Today it acts as a museum.

Height: 160 feet (16 stories tall)
Weight: 11 million pounds

Kansas is one of the top states for wheat production. Sometimes the state is called the Breadbasket of America.

The first Pizza Hut opened in Wichita in 1958.

Dwight Eisenhower's family moved to Abilene, Kansas, when he was very young. The future president lived there until he attended West Point. In a 1953 speech, he mentioned his hometown and its frontier past: "I was raised in a little town of which most of you have never heard. But in the West it is a famous place. … Now that town had a code, and I was raised as a boy to prize that code. It was: meet anyone face to face with whom you disagree."

Other Kansas firsts

NORTH DAKOTA

STRENGTH FROM THE SOIL

CAPITAL	Bismark
POPULATION	683,932
AREA	69,000 square miles
STATE FLOWER	Wild prairie rose
STATE FRUIT	Chokecherry

Theodore Roosevelt National Park

★ Bismark

The United States bought part of North Dakota, along with South Dakota, in the 1803 Louisiana Purchase. When Lewis and Clark began their expedition, they spent the winter of 1804-1805 in North Dakota, near the Mandan tribe. The first half of the century brought fur traders and military outposts to the region. The second half of the century brought ranchers and farmers drawn by the good soil. Dakota Territory was organized in 1861, and the Dakotas were made states in 1889.

The Enchanted Highway

In 1991, Gary Greff started putting up giant structures along a 32-mile stretch of road now called the Enchanted Highway. The sculptures are made of materials like old fuel tanks and used farm equipment.

A PRESIDENT OF PRESERVATION

Theodore Roosevelt lived as a rancher in Dakota Territory for several years. In his 1884 diary he wrote, "There are few sensations I prefer to that of galloping over these rolling, limitless prairies... or winding my way among the barren, fantastic, and grimly picturesque deserts of the so-called Bad Lands." Later, during his presidency, Roosevelt worked to set up national parks and preserve nature. The national park bearing his name is found in North Dakota.

North Dakota places

Theodore Roosevelt National Park

THE DAKOTAS LEAD THE COUNTRY IN SUNFLOWER PRODUCTION.

SOUTH DAKOTA
THE MOUNT RUSHMORE STATE

CAPITAL	Pierre
POPULATION	824,082
AREA	75,811 square miles
STATE ANIMAL	Coyote
STATE BREAD	Fry bread

Dakota gets its name from the Lakota word for "friend."

Make friends in... SOUTH Dakota

Like North Dakota, South Dakota was made part of Dakota Territory in 1861. Many settlers came to the plains to set up homes and farms. In 1874, an army expedition found gold in the Black Hills. Mining towns such as Deadwood sprang up. The Lakota fought to keep their land in the Black Hills, but they were forced onto reservations, as were other American Indians on the Great Plains. Today, agriculture and tourism are major industries in the state.

Mt. Rushmore
★ Pierre
Badlands
National Park

Good Views in the Badlands

Layers of rock built up in the Badlands over millions of years. Then wind and water began eroding those layers, leaving behind strange and beautiful formations. Badlands National Park is also a great place to find fossils.

More from the Badlands

A NATURAL PALACE

MITCHELL CORN PALACE
★America's Destinations★

The murals that decorate the Corn Palace in Mitchell are made from grains, grasses, and over 275,000 ears of corn! The murals change each year.

A corny puzzle

Out of the Rock

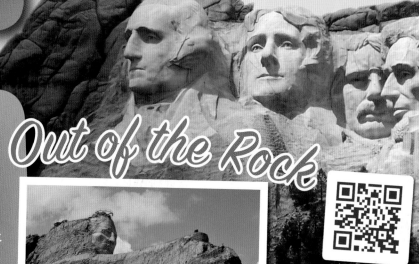

Between 1927 and 1941, a giant project took place in the Black Hills. Sculptor Gutzon Borglum and his team carved out four 60-foot tall presidential heads to make Mount Rushmore National Memorial: George Washington, Thomas Jefferson, Theodore Roosevelt, and Abraham Lincoln.

Another memorial is being carved out of a different mountain in the Black Hills. It honors the Lakota leader Crazy Horse. When finished, the sculpture will show the warrior on his horse.

South Dakota sculptures

Child of the Mississippi
LOUISIANA

UNION JUSTICE CONFIDENCE

In 1803, United States territory extended only to the Mississippi River. Then the United States bought a huge land area from France for $15 million. The purchase included the important port city of New Orleans. In 1812, Louisiana became the first state created from the territory.

Louisiana became a center of finance and trade early in its history. Its fertile farmlands made it a wealthy state. Indigo, sugar, and cotton crops made fortunes for many Louisiana planters. The plantation economy ended with the Civil War, but agriculture remained the backbone of the state. Lumber and oil became important new sources of wealth in the 20th century. Louisiana is now a major American producer of oil and natural gas.

CAPITAL	Baton Rouge
POPULATION	4,574,836
AREA	43,203 square miles
LARGEST CITY	New Orleans

THE BIRTHPLACE OF JAZZ

No American city has deeper jazz roots than New Orleans.

Louisiana Purchase 1803

Shreveport

Louisiana letter scramble!

Baton Rouge ★

New Orleans

CRAWFISH BOIL, ANYONE?

The state crustacean is found in marshes and swamps throughout the state. Louisianans love backyard crawfish boils, étouffée (a kind of stew), and bisque (a kind of soup).

Cajun Country

What's Cajun music?

Southern Louisiana's Cajuns are descendants of French settlers who came from eastern Canada in the 1700s. Today's Cajuns still speak a form of French and have their own special culture. Spicy dishes like *gumbo* and *jambalaya* are popular. Cajun music features accordion, fiddle, and lyrics sung in several languages.

What's cooking in New Orleans?

GUMBO!

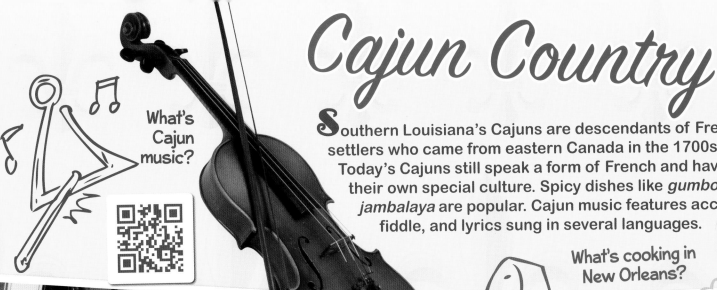

LOUISIANA FUN FACTS

NUMBER OF ISLANDS	2,482
NUMBER OF WILD ALLIGATORS	1.5–2 million
STATE MUSICAL INSTRUMENT	Cajun accordion
ORIGIN OF NAME	In honor of France's King Louis XIV
STATE BIRD	Eastern brown pelican
TOP AGRICULTURAL CROP	Lumber

The Louisiana state reptile is…

MARDI GRAS

Mardi Gras is one of the biggest celebrations in the country. It was brought to Louisiana long ago by the French. Over the years it became bigger and bigger. The New Orleans Mardi Gras now lasts about two weeks and attracts huge crowds from around the world.

Florida

THE SUNSHINE STATE

CAPITAL	Tallahassee
POPULATION	19,057,542
AREA	53,624 square miles
LARGEST CITY	Jacksonville

Florida was a Spanish territory until 1821, when it was acquired by the United States. It became a state in 1845. Florida draws tourists by the millions. They come to enjoy the warm sunshine, swaying palms, and beautiful beaches. They also come for amusement parks like Busch Gardens and Disney World.

Lots of people live in Florida year-round, too. There are more than 15 million Floridians. Most of them live in cities like Jacksonville and Miami. Florida has more senior citizens than any other state. Many people retire and move to Florida to enjoy the warmth and sun.

Florida state animals

Tallahassee
Jacksonville
Tampa
St. Petersburg
Lake Okeechobee
Miami
The Everglades

BALMY AND BREEZY
...usually

Florida has a *humid subtropical* climate. The weather is usually pleasant. But the annual hurricane season brings the risk of heavy winds and flooding.

A BEACH LOVER'S PARADISE

Florida has over 600 miles of coastal beaches. Florida's beaches are one reason over 80 million tourists visit the state each year.

The Everglades

IMAGINE TWO MILLION ACRES OF SWAMP!

The Everglades is made up of tropical hardwood and mangrove forests, saw grass marshes, and miles of shallow swamps and lakes. These wetlands stretch from the center of the state south to Florida Bay. The easiest way to get around is by kayak or airboat!

Here's a hint: It's also called a sea cow!

The Florida state marine mammal is...

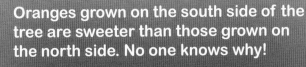

Oranges grown on the south side of the tree are sweeter than those grown on the north side. No one knows why!

State beverage: orange juice

Most important crop: oranges

90: percent of Florida oranges squeezed into juice

Number of orange trees: over 60 million

1513: year the Spanish brought oranges to Florida

AMERICA'S SPACEPORT

The Kennedy Space Center has been the launching pad for United States space flights since 1962.

Orange You Glad You Know?

Georgia
The Goober State

CAPITAL	Atlanta
POPULATION	9,815,210
AREA	57,513 square miles
YEAR OF STATEHOOD	1788

Europeans first came to Georgia in the mid-1500s and found American Indians already living there. English settlers arrived in 1733. They built Georgia's first town—Savannah. More settlers were attracted by the promise of religious freedom. At first the colony was sparsely settled. People grew rice and indigo and cut lumber. Settlers also traded for fur with American Indians.

Cotton was the most important crop in the state in the 19th century. The boll weevil arrived in 1915, and began to destroy cotton crops across the state. Farmers turned to other crops, like peanuts, peaches, and pecans. In the 20th century, textile manufacturing became the state's most important industry. Today the state is a major producer of carpets and clothing.

Georgia letter jumble!

Brasstown Bald

Atlanta

Savannah

Okefenokee Swamp

Atlanta

Land of the
TREMBLING EARTH

Travel to the southeast corner of Georgia, and you'll find a huge area covered with tea-colored water. This is the Okefenokee Swamp. Its name comes from a Seminole word and means "trembling earth." Why did the Seminoles call it that? The swamp is made of floating islands, which shake if you walk on them.

Okefenokee animals

WORLD'S LARGEST AQUARIUM

The Georgia Aquarium in Atlanta holds a total of eight million gallons of water. It has more aquatic life than any other aquarium in the world.

GEORGIA ON MY MIND

- Georgia has 144,000 acres of pecan trees.
- Georgia was named in honor of King George II of Britain.
- Highest point: Brasstown Bald (4,784 feet)
- Georgia makes over 80 percent of the carpet sold in the U.S.
- Official prepared food: grits
- At 700 square miles, Okefenokee Swamp is one of the biggest swamps in the country.
- State Pork Barbeque Championship Cook-off: The Slosheye Trail Big Pig Jig!

What's a Goober?

A goober is another name for a peanut. Georgia harvests about half of the country's peanut crop.

Where does peanut butter come from?

The Peach State

Georgia grows over 40 varieties of peaches.

Georgia quiz

The Blue Ridge Mountains

These mountains are part of the Appalachian chain that runs northeast from Alabama to Canada. They cover the northern part of Georgia.

SOUTH CAROLINA
The Palmetto State

CAPITAL	Columbia
POPULATION	4,679,230
AREA	30,060 square miles
STATE HOSPITALITY BEVERAGE	Tea

The Province of Carolina was divided into northern and southern colonies in 1712. Settlers from the Virginia Colony came to South Carolina for its rich soil and abundant timber. Its fertile coastal plain, known as the Low Country, was well-suited for growing indigo and rice. Cotton also became a major crop. Large plantations developed and made the colony wealthy. From the 1700s until the outbreak of the Civil War, South Carolina's plantation system, with its reliance on slave labor, helped the state's economy flourish.

After the war, South Carolina was faced with many economic and social challenges. The 1880s saw the emergence of its textile industry. After World War II, the manufacturing and tourism industries strengthened the economy further.

Historic Charleston

A STATELY TREE

The sabal palmetto is the state tree of South Carolina. It is represented on the state flag and seal. When the British attacked a South Carolina fort during the Revolutionary War, the cannonballs were absorbed by the fort's soft palmetto logs.

The Up Country

As you travel inland from the coastal plain, South Carolina's landscape changes to rolling hills. Farther west, the land grows more rugged as it approaches the Blue Ridge Mountains in the northwest corner of the state.

Table Rock State Park in the Blue Ridge Mountains

A Carolina conundrum

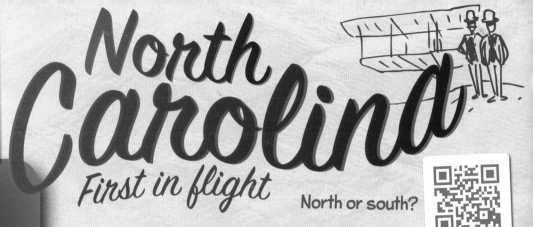

North Carolina
First in flight

North or south?

CAPITAL	Raleigh
POPULATION	9,656,401
AREA	48,617 square miles
STATE VEGETABLE	Sweet potato

North Carolina is the biggest producer of sweet potatoes in the country.

In 1789, North Carolina became the 12th of the original 13 colonies to gain statehood. Like other states of the coastal south, it developed its economy through agriculture. Rice, indigo, tobacco, and cotton were important crops.

North Carolina is now a major furniture and textile producer. The state's industry and population are concentrated in the Piedmont, in the middle of the state. Raleigh, the capital, and Charlotte, the biggest city, are in the Piedmont. The western part, with its rugged mountains, is more isolated. Mount Mitchell, at 6,684 feet, is the tallest peak in the eastern U.S.

Mount Mitchell • • Raleigh ★
Piedmont
Charlotte •
Outer Banks

TREACHEROUS WATERS

North Carolina's lovely coastline can be deadly. Its sandy shoals and islands, known as the Outer Banks, can change location over time. Thousands of ships have wrecked along the Outer Banks, earning the area the nickname "Graveyard of the Atlantic."

The Wright Flight

The Wright brothers came to a remote beach in the Outer Banks to test their ideas for mechanically propelled airplanes. In 1903, after four years of experimentation, they made history. The first airplane flight lasted 12 seconds and covered only 120 feet, but it signaled the beginning of the age of flight.

A great American drive

Bronze statues commemorate the first flight. The Wright Brothers National Memorial stands in the background.

TENNESSEE
A state of contrasts

Early pioneers came to Tennessee through the Cumberland Gap, a pass in the Cumberland Mountains where Tennessee, Kentucky, and Virginia meet. Many of these early settlers were from Virginia and the Carolinas. The land was cheap and the soil was fertile. By 1796, Tennessee had attracted enough settlers to become a state.

Tennessee has many contrasts. It extends from the mountainous North Carolina border in the east to Arkansas in the west. Farms cover about half of Tennessee's land. The most valuable farm product is beef. Other important crops include poultry, dairy products, soybeans, greenhouse products, cotton, and corn. The state's valuable natural resources include limestone and coal.

CAPITAL	Nashville
POPULATION	6,403,353
AREA	41,234 square miles
HIGHEST POINT	Clingmans Dome (6,643 feet)

Nashville ★   Knoxville •
Great Smoky Mountains
• Memphis   Chattanooga •

The Great Smoky Mountains, viewed from Clingmans Dome

STATEHOOD Key Dates

1763: The French surrender claims to lands east of the Mississippi to the British in the Treaty of Paris.

1763-1789: North Carolina controls the western land that will become Tennessee.

1775: Daniel Boone blazes Wilderness Road from Virginia through Cumberland Gap. Tennessee lands are opened for settlement.

1796: Tennessee becomes the 16th state of the Union.

1818: The state's western boundary is extended to the Mississippi River.

Tennessee trivia test!

Soulful Memphis

Music City, USA: Nashville

MUSIC: A Tale of Two Cities

Memphis and Nashville have deep roots in American music history. Memphis is known for its contributions to blues, rockabilly, rock 'n' roll, and soul. Nashville is known as the country music capital of the world.

THREE SUPER STARS

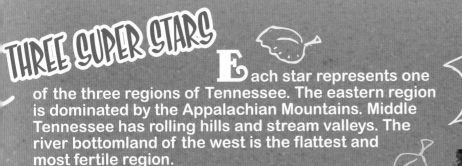

Each star represents one of the three regions of Tennessee. The eastern region is dominated by the Appalachian Mountains. Middle Tennessee has rolling hills and stream valleys. The river bottomland of the west is the flattest and most fertile region.

The Appalachian Trail

This 2,181-mile public footpath begins in Georgia and runs through 12 other states on its way to Maine. Some of the most scenic parts of the trail are in the Great Smoky Mountains, along the Tennessee and North Carolina border.

Mystery mark

THE STORY OF A NICKNAME

Tennessee earned the nickname "Volunteer State" during the War of 1812. Thousands of Tennesseans enlisted to help fight the British. The state supplied large numbers of volunteer soldiers for later wars too.

HOME OF THE KING

Elvis Presley's Graceland is a 20-minute drive from downtown Memphis. The white-columned mansion is now a museum. It preserves the interior just as it was at the time of Elvis's death in 1977.

KENTUCKY

The Bluegrass State

The state seal of Kentucky shows a frontiersman and a statesman shaking hands. The motto of Kentucky is "United We Stand, Divided We Fall."

Kentucky has a wild and wonderful history of exploration and development by many different people. American Indians were the first to explore its lands. Many tribes lived and hunted in its thick forests. In the 1700s, American colonists wanted to move west, but the Appalachian Mountains stood in their way. Thomas Walker's discovery of the Cumberland Gap on the western edge of Virginia gave them a new route into Kentucky and the Midwest.

Settlement was slow until the end of the Revolutionary War. After that, more settlers began to move to Kentucky. In 1792, Kentucky became the first state west of the Appalachian Mountains.

CAPITAL	Frankfort
POPULATION	4,369,356
AREA	39,486 square miles
LARGEST CITY	Louisville

Early History

1750	Thomas Walker passes through Cumberland Gap and explores Kentucky.
1774	Harrodsburg becomes Kentucky's first permanent settlement.
1792	Kentucky gains statehood.
1811	First steamboat on Ohio River reaches Louisville.
1818	Kentucky takes modern shape after western region annexed (Jackson Purchase).

WHAT DO YOU KNOW ABOUT KENTUCKY?

Louisville
★ Frankfort
Lexington

DANIEL BOONE
and the Wilderness Road

Daniel Boone was a famous frontiersman. In 1775, he blazed the trail that became known as the Wilderness Road. Beginning in Virginia, the road passed through the Cumberland Gap and wound through deep forests for 200 miles. It helped pioneers from eastern states reach Kentucky.

BLUE...GRASS?

Bluegrass is actually green. It gets its name because its spring flowers have a blue tint. Kentucky is known for its rolling fields and pastures of bluegrass.

MADE IN KENTUCKY

Horse farms dot the rolling green hills of Kentucky. The state's rich grasslands are good for raising horses.

Coal Country

Kentucky has two coal-producing regions: the large eastern region located along the Appalachians, and another large coal field on the western border. Coal has long been an important part of the Kentucky economy.

The Kentucky Derby

The Kentucky Derby takes place in Louisville every May. The first race was in 1875.

WHAT'S DOWN THERE?

Probably not him!

VIRGINIA
Mother of Presidents

CAPITAL	Richmond
POPULATION	8,096,604
AREA	39,490 square miles
HIGHEST POINT	Mt. Rogers (5,728 feet)

Shenandoah Valley

Richmond

Williamsburg

Jamestown

Mt. Rogers

Norfolk

Virginia Beach

In 1607, English colonists came to the shores of Virginia and established Jamestown. It was the first permanent English settlement in America. The early settlers planted wheat and corn for themselves and grew tobacco to trade with England for manufactured goods. Virginia was one of the 13 original colonies. It became a state in 1788, just five years after the end of the Revolutionary War.

People can see early Virginia history brought to life in Williamsburg. It is a restored colonial community. Visitors can eat at old inns and watch costumed workers practice old-fashioned trades like blacksmithing. They can see how the colonists lived and worked.

Virginia has many other historical sites. There are presidential landmarks such as Thomas Jefferson's Monticello, memorial sites like Arlington National Cemetery and Manassas National Battlefield Park, and also areas of great natural beauty. There are beautiful beaches and bays along the Atlantic Ocean. To the west are the Blue Ridge Mountains and the Shenandoah Valley.

The fertile Shenandoah Valley lies between the Blue Ridge Mountains and the Appalachians.

Colonial Williamsburg

Arlington National Cemetery's Tomb of the Unknowns

Name	Time in office
GEORGE WASHINGTON	1789 - 1797
THOMAS JEFFERSON	1801 - 1809
JAMES MADISON	1809 - 1817
JAMES MONROE	1817 - 1825
WILLIAM HENRY HARRISON	1841
JOHN TYLER	1841 - 1845
ZACHARY TAYLOR	1849 - 1850
WOODROW WILSON	1913 - 1921

OUR FIRST PRESIDENT

Mount Vernon was the home of George Washington. He was known as a political and military leader, but he was also an architect. He designed many of the buildings at Mount Vernon. The 500-acre estate is open to the public.

VIRGINIA'S BATTLEFIELDS

More Civil War battles were fought in Virginia than in any other state. Six national parks feature preserved battlefields, monuments, and memorials.

NAME THAT PRESIDENT!

Wild Ponies!

Wild ponies live on Assateague Island, on the Atlantic coast. They are descended from domesticated horses that grazed on the island 400 years ago.

WEST VIRGINIA
Wild and Wonderful

What do you know about WV?

CAPITAL	Charleston
POPULATION	1,855,364
AREA	24,038 square miles
STATE ROCK	Bituminous coal

West Virginia was once part of Virginia. During the Civil War, Virginia left the Union and joined the Confederacy. Many people in the western mountains of the state did not want to leave the Union. So West Virginians broke away from Virginia. In 1863, by proclamation of President Lincoln, West Virginia became the 35th state. It is the only state that has gained statehood this way.

West Virginia lies within the Appalachian Mountains. Its rugged hills and mountains make it a wonderful place to visit. There are many trails for hiking, and rivers for fishing and white-water rafting. Tourism is an important industry. Other major industries include coal mining, chemical manufacturing, and lumber production.

Appalachian flavor!

Morgantown

Huntington

★ Charleston

Monongahela National Forest

KING COAL

West Virginia's abundant coal was first noted in colonial times. By 1810, it was being commercially mined and sold for blacksmithing and domestic use. By 1860, there were 25 coal companies providing coal to steamboats, forges, and furnaces across the country. The state has been a major producer of coal ever since, and ranks second in yearly production.

Coal miners of the 19th century did much of their work with a pick and shovel.

Today, heavy machinery handles most coal extraction.

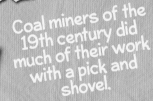

Shoot the Rapids!

If you like white-water rafting or kayaking, West Virginia is the place to go! Many of its rivers flow through a combination of peaceful pools, steep drops, and boulder-strewn rapids. It's a challenge that paddlers love!

ONE SONG IS NOT ENOUGH!

West Virginia has three official state songs. "West Virginia, My Home Sweet Home" was written in 1947. "This Is My West Virginia" was written in 1962. "The West Virginia Hills," probably the most popular, was written in 1885.

"The West Virginia Hills"

Monongahela National Forest

Date founded: 1920

Acres: over 919,000

Picnic areas: 17

Miles of hiking trails: over 500

Campgrounds: 23

West Virginia's state animal is the black bear. Many black bears live in Monongahela National Forest.

WEST VIRGINIA FUN FACTS

Nickname: The Mountain State

National parks: 6

West Virginia has the most irregular boundary of any state.

Percent of state electricity generated by coal: 99%

State reptile: Timber rattlesnake

The Natural State
ARKANSAS

CAPITAL	Little Rock
POPULATION	2,937,979
AREA	52,035 square miles
STATE MUSICAL INSTRUMENT	Fiddle

Arkansas was carved from the vast territory of the Louisiana Purchase. It became a territory in 1819 and a state in 1836. People came to Arkansas in the 1800s to work in the railroad, mining, and paper industries. Farming was also important. Today, Arkansas is known for its natural beauty as well as its natural resources. Visitors come to enjoy the forested mountains, hot springs, and waterfalls. Fishing, hunting, camping and boating are also popular.

Ozark Mountains

• Fort Smith

Little Rock ★

Pine Bluff

LITTLE ROCK

The capital of Arkansas was named for a small rock formation on the bank of the Arkansas River.

The White River in the Ozarks is just one place to enjoy nature in the Natural State.

A presidential puzzle

WHAT'S SO NATURAL ABOUT ARKANSAS?

An Agricultural Powerhouse

Arkansas leads the nation in rice production. It is number two in poultry and egg production and number three in aquaculture and turkeys.

MISSISSIPPI

MISSISSIPPI MAP CHALLENGE

CAPITAL	Jackson
POPULATION	2,978,512
AREA	46,923 square miles
YEAR OF STATEHOOD	1817

A great American river

Mississippi River

Jackson ★

Biloxi

Mississippi was the 20th state to join the Union. The state takes its name from the Mississippi River, which flows along its western border. It is a rural state, with about half of the population living in the country or in small towns.

Cotton was important to the state's development. Before the Civil War, there were many large, profitable cotton plantations. After the war, small farms replaced the plantations. Farming remained the main way of life until World War II helped ignite industrial growth. Today Mississippi is a balance of agriculture and industry.

The Mississippi River system covers about 40% of the lower 48 states. It is the fourth largest watershed in the world.

Drainage basin

MORE TOP CROPS

Corn

Soybeans

Cotton remains important to the state, with almost two million acres of the crop still planted.

Poultry

Aquaculture

MISSISSIPPI BLUES

Sweet Home... Alabama

Spanish explorers sailed into Mobile Bay in 1519. Hernando de Soto traveled through Alabama in 1540. For the next 250 years, the Spanish, the French, and the English fought over the area. Most of Alabama passed to the control of the United States after the American Revolution. Alabama became a state in 1819.

Alabama has been an agricultural state for much of its history. Its most important crop in the 19th century was cotton. To make cotton profitable, Alabama adopted the Virginia plantation system, organized around slave labor. Cotton was the major crop until about 1915, when the boll weevil arrived. This pest forced farmers to raise crops other than cotton—ultimately making their farms more profitable. Today, Alabama has a diverse agricultural economy. Cotton now represents less than 4 percent of the state's farm output.

CAPITAL	Montgomery
POPULATION	4,802,740
AREA	50,645 square miles
LARGEST CITY	Birmingham

STATE BIRD: YELLOWHAMMER

FROM SMOKY HILLS TO SUGAR SANDS

Birmingham

Montgomery ★

Mobile

The boll weevil

WHAT DO YOU KNOW ABOUT ALABAMA?

The state capitol building in Montgomery

Welcome to

Alabama the Beautiful

ONLY IN ALABAMA

- The Boll Weevil Monument in the town of Enterprise is dedicated to the bug. The pest that destroyed Alabama's cotton crops a century ago is now remembered with gratitude.

- Alabama has an official outdoor musical drama. It is called "The Incident at Looney's Tavern."

- In Scottsboro, the Unclaimed Baggage Center sells items lost on buses, trains, and airlines from all over the country. The building is larger than a city block.

- The only state containing all the major natural resources for making iron and steel is Alabama.

- Huntsville is home to NASA's Marshall Space Flight Center. The Saturn V rocket that put humans on the moon was built here.

- The town of Magnolia Springs receives its mail in a unique way—by boat!

AVERAGE FARM SIZE: ABOUT 186 ACRES

State border bingo!

Unusual Places

THAT'S A LOT OF CHICKENS!

Broilers (young chickens grown for cooking) make up most of Alabama's livestock production. There are about 108 million broilers in Alabama—that's 23 times more chickens than Alabamians!

OTHER TOP CROPS

Eggs

Greenhouse/nursery

Peanuts

Aquaculture

Livestock

Dairy

Corn

USA

It's OK in... Oklahoma

OKLAHOMA

Oklahoma was bought by the United States in 1803 as part of the Louisiana Purchase. Several American Indian tribes lived in the area already, including the Comanche, Osage, and Kiowa. The decades that followed brought many more tribes. Tribes like the Cherokee, Seminole, Chickasaw, Choctaw, and Creek were forced to move from the eastern parts of the United States to the area then known as Indian Territory.

In 1889, the U.S. federal government opened part of the region to white settlement. Settlers poured into the area. In 1907, Oklahoma Territory and Indian Territory were joined into the state of Oklahoma.

Do you know Oklahoma?

CAPITAL	Oklahoma City
POPULATION	3,791,508
AREA	68,595 square miles
STATE ANIMAL	Buffalo
STATE FLOWER	Oklahoma rose

The official state meal

Tulsa

Oklahoma City ★

THE SOONER STATE

The first land run took place on April 22, 1889. Thousands of settlers gathered to wait until noon. Then they rushed into Oklahoma to find a piece of land on which to make a claim. Other land runs followed. One of the biggest, shown below, took place in 1893. Sometimes people snuck in early to get the best land. They were called Sooners, and the state nickname became "The Sooner State."

Oklahoma's neighbors

An oil pump

Wild Weather

Oklahoma is part of the region known as Tornado Alley. Between 1950 and 2011, Oklahoma had over 3,400 recorded tornadoes. Here are some of the deadliest and costliest tornadoes in Oklahoma history:

MAY 10, 1905

Two years before Oklahoma became a state, this tornado hit the southwest part of Oklahoma Territory. An estimated death toll of 97 makes this the second-deadliest tornado in Oklahoma history.

APRIL 9, 1947

The deadliest tornado in Oklahoma destroyed over 100 city blocks in the town of Woodward. One hundred sixteen people were killed.

MAY 3, 1999

In May 1999, 90 tornadoes were recorded in Oklahoma. Many were part of a tornado outbreak that hammered the region in early May. One F5 tornado that hit Oklahoma City cost over $1 billion in damages.

The Wichita Mountains Wildlife Refuge

AN OKLAHOMA RECORD

Oklahoma has more man-made lakes than any other state.

BLACK GOLD

The oil industry has a long history in Oklahoma. In 1859, people drilling for salt found oil instead! The state's first commercial oil well was completed in 1897. In the early 1900s, Oklahoma was the top state for oil production, and oil has remained a critical industry.

The Golden Driller, the state monument, celebrates this aspect of Oklahoma's history. At 76 feet tall and with a weight of 43,500 pounds, it's the largest free-standing statue in the world.

SOME OK INVENTIONS

Oklahoma saw the birth of some inventions that we use everyday.

What: The parking meter
When and where: 1935 in Oklahoma City
Cost: One nickel per hour

What: The shopping cart
When and where: 1937 in Oklahoma City
Patented as: Folding basket carriage for self-service stores

What: The first Yield sign
When and where: 1950 in Tulsa, Oklahoma
The first signs said: Yield Right of Way

The Lone Star State

TEXAS

CAPITAL	Austin
POPULATION	25,674,681
AREA	261,232 square miles
STATE SMALL MAMMAL	Armadillo
STATE FOOTWEAR	Cowboy boot

The state large mammal

Amarillo

Dallas

Fort Worth

El Paso

Austin

Houston

San Antonio

Corpus Christi

In the 1500s, the Spanish were the first Europeans to claim Texas. Aside from a brief period in the late 1600s when the French tried to settle the area, Spanish rule continued until 1821. Then Mexico became independent from Spain. Texas was a state within Mexico.

However, Americans were also settling there. The Texans began to clash with the Mexican government. They wanted more independence, and they fought for it. From 1836 to 1845, the Republic of Texas governed itself. Then, in 1845, Texas entered the United States.

Remember the Alamo

HOW MANY BATS?

Between March and November, the city of Austin is the place to go if you want to see a bat—or 1.5 million of them. A colony of Mexican free-tailed bats spends those months living under the Congress Avenue Bridge. Each evening, they fly away from the bridge to find insects to eat.

EXTREME WEATHER

GREATEST U.S. RAINFALL IN A 24-HOUR PERIOD

42 inches fell on Alvin, Texas during Tropical Storm Claudette in 1979.

DEADLIEST HURRICANE IN U.S. HISTORY

In 1900, a level 4 hurricane hit the island of Galveston. High tides flooded the island. More than 6,000 residents were killed.

BARRELS OF BUSINESS

Texas oil production began on a small scale in the late 1800s. It boomed in 1901 when a well at Spindletop Hill started gushing oil into the air. It took nine days to get the well under control! In 1902, the Spindletop Hill site produced 17.5 million barrels of oil. Today, Texas is the top state in oil production. It produces over a million barrels a day.

FAMOUS TEXANS

RACING TO SPACE

Mission Control

Based in Houston, the Johnson Space Center is NASA's headquarters for human spaceflight exploration. The center trains astronauts and acts as Mission Control.

COWBOYS AND RODEOS

Visit a Texas rodeo to see bull riding, bucking broncos, and cattle roping!

WHAT DO YOU KNOW?

Amarillo is the home of a famous roadside landmark: 10 Cadillacs partly buried in the ground. This piece of public art is interactive. People are encouraged to spray paint and add graffiti.

Cadillac Ranch

New Mexico

Land of Enchantment

The highest capital city with an elevation of over 7,000 feet.

CAPITAL	Santa Fe
POPULATION	2,082,224
AREA	121,298 square miles
STATE GEM	Turquoise
STATE BIRD	Greater roadrunner

New Mexico is a blend of several different cultures. American Indians have lived in the region for at least 10,000 years. The Spanish began to settle in the area in the 1500s. The area became part of Mexico in 1821, after Mexico declared independence from Spain. In 1848, the territory entered the United States as a result of the Mexican-American War. New Mexico became the 47th state in 1912.

See the state bird

Bandelier National Monument
Taos Pueblo
★ Santa Fe
Petroglyph National Monument
Albuquerque
Carlsbad Caverns

A LONG HISTORY

The Taos American Indians and their ancestors have lived in Taos Pueblo for a long time. Some parts of the adobe buildings date back one thousand years.

The Palace of the Governors in Santa Fe was built in 1610 by the Spanish. It served as the seat of government for the region. Today it's a museum.

At Petroglyph National Monument, visitors can see rock carvings, or petroglyphs, created by the Ancestral Puebloans.

More petroglyphs

Ancestral Puebloans lived in the area that is now Bandelier National Monument from 1100 to 1550. They left behind dwellings and rock art.

TAKING TO THE SKIES

Each autumn, hot air balloons fill the skies over Albuquerque during Albuquerque's International Balloon Fiesta.

WHAT DO YOU KNOW?

RED OR GREEN?

That's the official state question of New Mexico. It asks what kind of chile sauce you want on top of your food. The chile is one of New Mexico's state vegetables, along with frijoles (beans).

CARLSBAD CAVERNS

Around 1900, cowboy Jim White saw a lot of bats rising out of a hole in the ground. He began to explore the place where the bats had come from. Later, he guided other explorers through the ancient cave system. Today, visitors go to Carlsbad Caverns National Park to see the incredible cave formations—and the bats!

See more of the caves

750 POUNDS OF CORN

50 POUNDS OF CHOPPED ONIONS

175 POUNDS OF CHEESE

75 GALLONS OF RED CHILE SAUCE

What could you make with those ingredients? Each year, people in Las Cruces make a giant enchilada as part of the Whole Enchilada Festival.

A grand adventure...
ARIZONA

Arizona has a long history of human settlement by the Hopi, Navajo, Apache, and other American Indian tribes. The Spanish began to explore and settle the area in the 1500s. The area then became part of Mexico. The United States gained control of most of the land in 1848, as a result of the Mexican-American War. It bought the rest in 1853. However, Arizona did not become a state until 1912.

CAPITAL	Phoenix
POPULATION	6,482,505
AREA	113,594 square miles
STATE FLOWER	Saguaro cactus blossom
STATE AMPHIBIAN	Arizona tree frog

Grand Canyon

Navajo Nation

Phoenix ★

Tucson

NAVAJO NATION

Many American Indian reservations are found in Arizona, including the Navajo Nation, the largest in the country. Some Navajo men played an important part in World War II. These soldiers served as "code talkers" in the Marine Corps. Their code, based on the Navajo language, was never cracked by Axis forces.

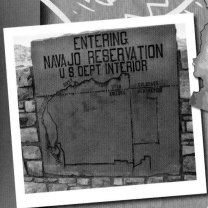

ENTERING NAVAJO RESERVATION U.S. DEPT. INTERIOR

Natural Wonders

Arizona is the home to many natural wonders, including the vast expanse of the Grand Canyon.

Depth: **One mile**

Width: **18 miles at its widest point**

Length: **277 miles**

Formed by: **The Colorado River**

See the canyon

More natural wonders

Canyon scramble

UNUSUAL ARIZONA

Biosphere 2 has small versions of some of Earth's ecosystems: a rainforest, a swamp, grasslands, and more.

This may look like a giant sculpture, but it is actually a restaurant, the Longhorn Grill.

Race to Chandler, Arizona, to see its yearly Ostrich Festival, complete with ostrich races.

About 50,000 years ago, a meteorite hit the ground in what is now Winslow, Arizona. It left a crater 4,000 feet in diameter and about 550 feet deep.

DUEL in the DESERT

In a famous rivalry, football teams from the University of Arizona and Arizona State University meet once a year to compete. They first met on the field in 1899!

Famous Arizonans

THE SAGUARO CACTUS

In southwestern Arizona's Sonoran Desert, travelers can see the largest cacti in the United States. The saguaro cactus grows slowly. In the first 10 years of its life, the cactus only grows about an inch. Later in life, it towers 40 to 60 feet. It doesn't bloom until it is 50 or 75 years old.

Four Corners

Want to visit four states in less than a minute? Take a quick walk around Four Corners Monument, the only point in the United States where four states meet: Utah, Colorado, New Mexico, and Arizona.

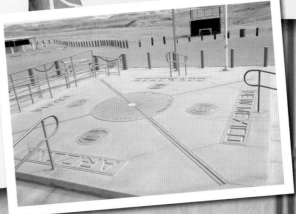

THE SILVER STATE
Nevada

Nevada knowledge

Americans began travelling through and settling in Nevada in the 1840s and 1850s. In 1859, silver was discovered at the Comstock Lode. The area boomed. Nevada quickly became a territory in 1861, and the 36th state in 1864. Gold and silver mining were important industries. In fact, a mint was established in Carson City. Gold mining is still an important industry today, as is tourism.

CAPITAL	Carson City
POPULATION	2,723,322
AREA	109,781 square miles
STATE TREE	Bristlecone pine
STATE BIRD	Mountain bluebird

Reno
★ Carson City

Las Vegas

Hoover Dam

The Bellagio fountains

LAS VEGAS

The city of Las Vegas attracts many tourists for its themed hotels, shows, rides, and more.

See famous figures at the wax museum, Madame Tussauds.

Nevada is the #1 state for gold production.

ANCIENT HUNTERS

Archaeologists have found duck decoys in Nevada that date back about 2,000 years. The decoys were used while hunting. They drew in real birds.

"This Great Feat"

Hoover Dam, found on the Arizona-Nevada border, provides power to those states and parts of California.

Size: 726 feet high by 1,244 feet long
Thickness of its base: 660 feet
Dedicated: 1935

President Franklin Delano Roosevelt's words at the dedication: "This morning I came, I saw, and I was conquered, as everyone would be who sees for the first time this great feat of mankind."

Mormon settlers wanted to call the state Deseret, meaning honeybee.

The Beehive State

UTAH

CAPITAL	Salt Lake City
POPULATION	2,817,222
AREA	82,170 square miles
STATE MINERAL	Copper
STATE INSECT	Honeybee

Do you know Utah?

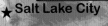

★ Salt Lake City

• Provo

Arches National Park•

In 1847, Brigham Young, the head of the Church of Jesus Christ of Latter-day Saints, brought a group of Mormons to settle near the Great Salt Lake. They wanted to live someplace where they could practice their religion freely. At the time, Utah was part of Mexico. In 1848, however, Utah became part of the United States after the Mexican-American War. Mormons continued to move to the area. Miners also began to come to the region. In 1896, Utah became the 45th state.

OLYMPIC PARK

In 2002, Utah hosted the Winter Olympics. Events like ski jumping, luge, and bobsled were hosted at Olympic Park. Today tourists visit for fun, while athletes go there to train.

Bobsledding

The Golden Spike

In the 1860s, railroad tracks were being built from the east and from the west. In 1869, they met in Promontory, Utah. When the last spike was hammered in, the transcontinental railroad was complete.

A Very Big Pit

The Bingham Canyon Mine has produced more than 19 million tons of copper. It is three-quarters of a mile deep.

Arches National Park

I'd go to... Idaho

#1 state in potato production!

CAPITAL	Boise
POPULATION	1,584,985
AREA	82,643 square miles
STATE VEGETABLE	Potato
STATE HORSE	Appaloosa

Idaho became part of the United States in 1846, when the United States signed the Oregon Treaty with Britain. In the 1860s, American miners came to the area. As more Americans settled, they had more conflicts with American Indian tribes. The Nez Percé and the Bannocks warred with the federal government in the 1870s. They lost their fight. In 1890, Idaho became the 43rd state.

ANCIENT ANIMALS

Hagerman Fossil Beds National Monument is full of fossils. Scientists have found camels, sloths, and over two hundred examples of the Hagerman Horse. These animals, closer to a modern zebra, lived about 3.5 million years ago.

CRATERS OF THE MOON

The landscape of this national monument was shaped by volcanic activity. There are craters, lava fields, and lava tubes and caves. The *Apollo 14* astronauts came here before their mission for some geological training.

Lava

Which state?

Idaho's lakes and rivers

Boise ★

Craters of the Moon National Monument •

Hagerman Fossil Beds National Monument •

Explorer and Guide

Sacagawea, who acted as a guide on the Lewis and Clark expedition, was a Shoshone woman. Her people lived near what is now the border between Idaho and Montana. Sacagawea acted as an interpreter for the Corps of Discovery. She also knew which plants were safe to eat. A few months before the expedition began, Sacagawea became a mother, and she took her baby boy on the trip!

MONTANA

Big sky country

MONTANA

CAPITAL	Helena
POPULATION	998,199
AREA	145,546 square miles
STATE GEMS	Sapphires and agates
STATE BUTTERFLY	Mourning cloak

In 1803, the Louisiana Purchase brought most of the area now known as Montana to the United States. Fur traders and then ranchers began to settle in the area. In 1862, gold was discovered. Cities like Helena and Butte began as mining towns for gold and silver. Montana became the 41st state in 1889.

Great Falls

Helena

Billings Little Bighorn Battlefield National Monument

THE BATTLE OF LITTLE BIGHORN

In 1876, the U.S. Army was at war with several American Indian tribes. The Lakota, Cheyenne, and Arapaho did not want to leave their ancestral lands. In June 1876, a famous battle was fought. The American Indians, led by Sitting Bull and Crazy Horse, won. The battle was also called Custer's Last Stand after the leader of the American troops. Today, the battlefield has memorials for the soldiers on both sides.

RUNNING HOT AND COLD

Montana's lowest recorded temperature
January 1954
-70°F

Montana's highest recorded temperature
July 1937
117°F

Montana wildlife

EGG MOUNTAIN

In the late 1970s, a new species of dinosaur was discovered in Montana, a plant-eating dinosaur called Maiasaura. At one site called Egg Mountain, archaeologists found rare fossils of eggs and young dinosaurs as well as adults.

Montana's neighbors

On the big plains...
WYOMING

Letter scramble

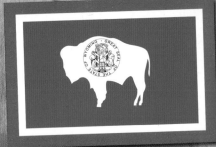

Wyoming became part of the United States with the 1803 Louisiana Purchase, and American explorers and fur trappers began to visit the area. In the 1820s and 1830s, these "mountain men" met once a year in Wyoming to sell their furs to traders and have a party. Other settlers came slowly to the area. Wyoming became a territory in 1868 and a state in 1890.

CAPITAL	Cheyenne
POPULATION	568,158
AREA	97,093 square miles
STATE SPORT	Rodeo
STATE DINOSAUR	Triceratops

Least populated state. There are about 65 times more people in California than Wyoming.

WYOMING WONDERS

Created in 1872, Yellowstone National Park was the first national park. It has close to 300 waterfalls and over 300 geysers, many animals, and one active volcano.

A famous geyser!

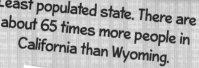

Yellowstone National Park

Casper

Cheyenne

Women in Wyoming

American women fought for the right to vote and the right to hold public office for a long time. Wyoming was one of the first places to acknowledge those rights.

1869: The territory of Wyoming grants women the vote.

1870: Wyoming appoints the nation's first female justice of the peace, Esther Morris.

1890: Wyoming becomes a state, the first where women can vote.

1893: Colorado passes an amendment to become the second state to grant women the right to vote.

1920: Women are guaranteed the right to vote throughout the United States.

Wyoming is the leading state in coal production. About 40% of U.S. coal is produced there.

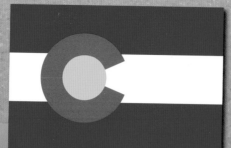

Colorado

CAPITAL	Denver
POPULATION	5,116,796
AREA	103,642 square miles
STATE ANIMAL	Rocky Mountain bighorn sheep
STATE FOSSIL	Stegosaurus

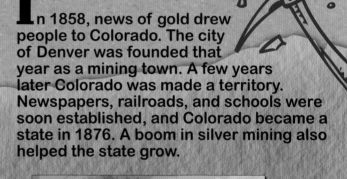

In 1858, news of gold drew people to Colorado. The city of Denver was founded that year as a mining town. A few years later Colorado was made a territory. Newspapers, railroads, and schools were soon established, and Colorado became a state in 1876. A boom in silver mining also helped the state grow.

Colorado draws people in the winter months for its many winter sports, including skiing, snowboarding, and ice climbing.

Skiing in Colorado

Denver

Colorado Springs

Mesa Verde National Park

Colorado quiz

EXTREME ELEVATION

Denver, called the Mile High City for its elevation above sea level, is one of the country's highest capitals. Colorado sets some of the country's height records.

Highest incorporated city
Leadville, a former mining town, has an elevation of 10,152 feet.

Highest paved road
The Mount Evans Scenic Byway reaches an altitude of over 14,000 feet.

Highest tunnel open for vehicles
The highest point on the Interstate Highway System is named after the president who founded that system. Eisenhower Tunnel runs through the Rocky Mountains at a height of over 11,000 feet.

Home Sweet Home

About 1,400 years ago, a group of Ancestral Puebloans settled in the cliffs of Mesa Verde. They lived in the region for about 700 years before moving south, and left behind the dwellings they had built out of the cliffs.

More from Mesa Verde

Coins stamped with the letter D are made in the Denver Mint.

THE GOLDEN STATE
California

CALIFORNIA REPUBLIC

California was originally home to many different groups of American Indians. European settlers began to arrive in the 1500s. In the 1700s and 1800s, Spanish priests built missions up and down the coastline. The missions were shut down when California became part of Mexico, but some of the buildings remain as historical landmarks today. The year 1848 brought two big changes to California. The area became part of United States territory as a result of the Mexican-American War. And gold was discovered. People flocked to the area in search of wealth. California became a state two years later.

Redwood National Forest

Sacramento

San Francisco
Oakland
San Jose

Yosemite National Park

Fresno

Mt. Whitney
Death Valley

Los Angeles
Anaheim
Long Beach
Santa Ana
San Diego

CAPITAL	Sacramento
POPULATION	37,691,912
AREA	155,779 square miles
STATE DANCE	West Coast Swing

Biggest state population!

Other state symbols

RECORD-SETTING CALIFORNIA

Highest recorded temperature in the U.S.: In 1913, the temperature in Death Valley in the Mojave Desert reached 134 degrees Fahrenheit, or 57 degrees Celsius.

World's tallest tree: Some coast redwoods in Redwood National Park top 370 feet, or 112 meters. That's longer than an American football field.

Lowest place in the U.S.: Death Valley wins this record as well. The lowest spot is 282 feet below sea level.

Highest mountain in the 48 contiguous states: Mount Whitney, found less than 100 miles away from Death Valley, rises about 14,500 feet.

Famous Californians

First solar-powered Ferris wheel: The first—and so far only—solar-powered Ferris wheel is found at Pacific Park, an amusement park on Santa Monica pier.

California quiz

REACHING FOR THE STARS

Sally Ride, the first American woman to enter space, was born in Encino, California.

Go for the Gold

YOSEMITE NATIONAL PARK

California's many national parks play a part in preserving the state's beauty. One well-known park is Yosemite, which has many natural wonders: giant sequoia trees, many water-falls, and the great granite monolith called Half Dome.

California's national parks

The Gold Rush lasted less than a decade, but it changed California forever. Migrants came from the eastern and midwestern states, from Mexico, and from China. Even after the Gold Rush ended, the state continued to grow. However, some former mining sites were left as ghost towns. Bodie is now the official state Gold Rush ghost town.

1848: Gold is discovered at Sutter's Mill

7,000: The number of people who rushed to the area in 1848

100,000: The number of people who rushed to the area in 1849

49ers: The name given to the migrants who came to California in 1849 (And the name of San Francisco's football team!)

300,000: Estimated number of people who came to the state overall (although not everyone stayed)

Bodie, CA

In the 1910s, studios began moving to Los Angeles to take advantage of California's sunny weather. Hollywood became the center of America's film industry. The first stars on Hollywood's Walk of Fame were given in 1960. Today, about 2,500 people and groups from the entertainment industry are honored.

THE WALK OF FAME

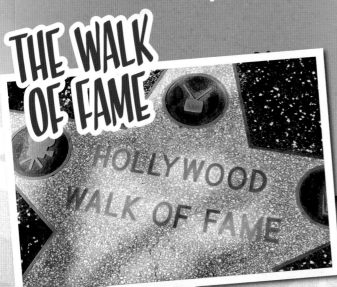
HOLLYWOOD WALK OF FAME

Van Ness Ave., California
49
Market Streets

San Francisco's cable cars began running in the 1870s.

On the trail to... Oregon

Oregon's flag has two sides!

CAPITAL	Salem
POPULATION	3,871,859
AREA	95,988 square miles
STATE BEVERAGE	Milk
STATE BIRD	Western meadowlark

In November 1805, Lewis and Clark's famous expedition reached its westward point at the mouth of the Columbia River, near present-day Astoria, Oregon. The explorers built a fort and spent the winter there before beginning their trip home. The decades that followed brought many settlers to Oregon and the Pacific Northwest. Both British and American settlers came in the first half of the 19th century. Then, in 1846, the Oregon Treaty was signed, marking the border between British and American land. In 1848, the U.S. government formed the Oregon Territory. It included the areas that are now Oregon, Washington, Idaho, and parts of Montana and Wyoming. The state of Oregon was created in 1859.

Before a transcontinental railroad was finished in 1869, American settlers to the Pacific Northwest usually followed a land route called the Oregon Trail. A group of over one thousand settlers made the first big migration in 1843. In the decades that followed, thousands more made their way west along the Oregon Trail.

The Oregon Trail

Columbia River
Portland
Salem
Crater Lake

INTO THE DEPTHS

Crater Lake, located in Crater Lake National Park in the southwest corner of the state, is the country's deepest lake. The lake was created more than 7,000 years ago when a volcano collapsed, leaving a giant crater behind. Its water is very pure, which helps the lake keep its deep blue color.

CRATER LAKE 1,932 FEET	LAKE SUPERIOR 1,332 FEET	LAKE MICHIGAN 925 FEET	LAKE ERIE 210 FEET	GREAT SALT LAKE 34 FEET

500 FT
1,000 FT
1,500 FT
2,000 FT

Stop to Smell the Roses

Visitors have been enjoying the sight and smell of roses in Portland's International Rose Test Garden since 1917.

- Over 500 varieties
- About 10,000 plants
- A Rose Festival is held each summer
- Portland's nickname: City of Roses

THE COLUMBIA RIVER GORGE

Formed by the Columbia River, this canyon stretches over 80 miles of natural beauty. Some parts of the gorge are especially popular with windsurfers and kitesurfers. The Columbia River Gorge is known for its many waterfalls. Multnomah Falls, one of the most notable waterfalls in the U.S., cascades down 620 feet over two levels.

See the Falls

SOME FAMOUS OREGONIANS

MATT GROENING

Famous cartoonist and creator of *The Simpsons*

Born in Portland

BEVERLY CLEARY

Author of many children's books, including the Beezus and Ramona series

Born in McMinnville

LINUS PAULING

Chemist, winner of two Nobel Prizes

Born in Portland

KNOW YOUR STATE SYMBOLS

GASOLINE

FIRE-CHIEF

THIS SALE $ 0 0 0
Wayne
0 0 0 GALLONS
0 0 0 CENTS PER GALLON

Wayne

FIRE-CHIEF GASOLINE

Oregon is one of two states without self-serve gas stations.

Westward to... WASHINGTON

Only state named after a president

CAPITAL	Olympia
POPULATION	6,830,038
AREA	66,456 square miles
STATE VEGETABLE	Walla Walla sweet onion
STATE FISH	Steelhead trout

Olympic National Park

Seattle

Olympia

Mt. St. Helens

Columbia River

The late 1700s and early 1800s were a time of change and conflict in the Pacific Northwest. Spain, Britain, the United States, and local American Indian tribes all had interests and competing claims in the region. As the 1800s continued, British and American settlement increased, driven by the fur trade. In 1846, Britain and the United States signed the Oregon Treaty. It divided the land they were arguing about along the 49th parallel. Washington was on the U.S. side of the line. In the years that followed, American Indian tribes lost land through treaties and wars. In 1889, Washington was made the 42nd state.

WHAT DO YOU KNOW?

WASHINGTON WONDERS

Scenes from the park

Olympic National Park offers 1,440 square miles of natural beauty, including mountains, coastline, and rare temperate rain forests.

Washington grows more apples than any other state.

MOUNT ST. HELENS

In Spring 1980, the area around Mount St. Helens had a series of earthquakes. The mountain began to change shape because of gathering magma. On May 18, an earthquake triggered a massive landslide. An explosive eruption followed. Forests, homes, bridges, and highways were destroyed.

BOOMING BUSINESS

Some very well-known companies are associated with the state of Washington.

AMAZON Amazon.com was incorporated in Washington in 1994. Headquartered in Seattle, the company now has over 65,000 employees worldwide.

BOEING Boeing was founded in Seattle in 1916. In 1968, the first 747 was manufactured in an assembly plant in Everett, Washington. Jumbo jets are still manufactured there today.

COSTCO In 1983, the first Costco warehouse opened in Seattle. Now headquartered in Issaquah, Washington, Costco has almost 600 locations.

MICROSOFT In 1979, Microsoft headquarters moved from New Mexico to Bellevue, Washington. Their current headquarters in Redmond cover over 300 acres of land.

STARBUCKS Starbucks has over 15,000 locations today, but the company began as a single coffee shop in Seattle in 1971.

Flying high

Seattle sights

The Space Needle, **605 feet tall,** *was built for the 1962 World's Fair.*

WATERPOWER

The Grand Coulee Dam on the Columbia River provides hydroelectric power to eleven states.

- CONSTRUCTION: 1933-1942, 1969-1974
- LARGEST HYDROPOWER PRODUCER IN THE U.S.
- LARGEST CONCRETE DAM IN THE U.S.

North to the future...
ALASKA

In 1867, Russia owned Alaska. They offered to sell it to the United States, and Secretary of State William Seward made the purchase. The cost was 7.2 million dollars—a low price for such a big piece of land. Still, Seward's political opponents protested the decision. They called it Seward's Folly. Later, gold was discovered, and many people suddenly saw Alaska's value. Alaska became a territory in 1912 and the 49th state in 1959.

CAPITAL	Juneau
POPULATION	722,718
AREA	570,641 square miles
STATE FOSSIL	Woolly mammoth
STATE SPORT	Dog mushing

The Iltarod

Fairbanks

Mt. McKinley

Anchorage

Juneau

Travel in Alaska

ALASKA RECORDS

LARGEST STATE
Alaska is more than 500 times the size of Rhode Island!

MOST POWERFUL U.S. EARTHQUAKE
The 1964 Alaskan Earthquake measured 9.2 on the Richter scale.

TALLEST MOUNTAINS
The 10 tallest mountains in the U.S. are all found in Alaska. The tallest, Mount McKinley, or Denali, measures 20,320 feet.

NORTHERNMOST U.S. CITY
Barrow, Alaska. In the far north, winter days are very short and summer days very long. Barrow is so far north that for over 60 days in the winter months, the sun does not rise over the horizon. In summer, the sun does not fully set for over 80 days.

ICY ART

Each winter, the city of Fairbanks hosts the World Ice Art championships. Artists compete by carving sculptures from giant blocks of ice. Kids can play in a park with slides and mazes made from ice.

Alaska vs. Hawaii

Aloha HAWAII

CAPITAL	Honolulu
POPULATION	1,374,810
AREA	6,423 square miles
STATE MARINE MAMMAL	Humpback whale

The state of Hawaii has one hundred thirty-two islands, although most people live on the eight main islands. King Kamehameha I, honored on the state quarter, united the Hawaiian Islands under his rule in the early 1800s. The last monarch of Hawaii, Queen Liliʻuokalani, was overthrown by foreign business executives in 1893. They wanted Americans to run the country. In 1898, the U.S. Congress formally annexed Hawaii. It became the 50th state in 1959.

NIHAU • KAUAI • OAHU • Honolulu • MOLOKAI • LANAI • KAHOOLAWE • MAUI • HAWAII • Mauna Kea • Mauna Loa • Kilauea

Traditional dance

At the Polynesian Cultural Center on Oahu, people perform the traditional songs, chants, and dances from the Pacific Islands.

Surfing is the state's official individual sport. Oahu's popular North Shore gets its biggest waves during the winter months.

Surfers at Oahu

LOOKING AT LAVA

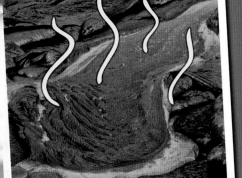

The Hawaiian Islands were formed through volcanic activity. The islands we see are just the tips of mountains that rise from the ocean floor. Some of the most remarkable volcanoes are found on the Big Island.

MAUNA KEA
Status: Has not erupted for thousands of years
Tallest volcano

MAUNA LOA
Status: Active
Largest volcano

KILAUEA
Status: Active
Has erupted continuously since 1983

What Do You Know About the UNITED STATES?

STATE CAPITAL REVIEW

Nicknames and mottos

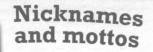

Landmarks and national parks

U.S. facts

Bodies of water

State statistics

Symbols

Natural features

Forming the Union

Flags and songs

Map labels

Washington, Montana, North Dakota, Minnesota, Maine, Vermont, Oregon, Idaho, Rocky Mountains, South Dakota, Wisconsin, Michigan, New York, New Hampshire, Massachusetts, Rhode Island, Connecticut, Pennsylvania, New Jersey, Delaware, Maryland, Washington, D.C., Wyoming, Iowa, Nevada, Nebraska, Illinois, Indiana, Ohio, West Virginia, Virginia, Appalachian Mountains, California, Utah, Colorado, Kansas, Missouri, Kentucky, North Carolina, Arizona, New Mexico, Oklahoma, Arkansas, Tennessee, South Carolina, Alaska, Mississippi River, Mississippi, Alabama, Georgia, Texas, Louisiana, Florida, Hawaii